Guidebook:
three manœuvres by Tim Brennan in London E1/E2

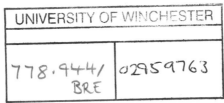

Guidebook:
three manœuvres by Tim Brennan
in London E1/E2

A *Camerawords* publication
edited by Tim Brennan & Geoff Cox, Volume 2

First published in 1999 by
Camerawork
121 Roman Road, London E2
tel: 0181 980 6256
distributed by Cornerhouse

Printed in UK by Spiderweb Ltd.

ISBN 1 871103 12 6

GUIDEBOOK:
three manœuvres by Tim Brennan
in London E1/E2

contents: p.

ACKNOWLEDGEMENTS

Thanks to Combined Arts Department, London Arts Board; Royal London Hospital; Bethnal Green Museum of Childhood; John Gange; Hiroko Sometani; Sandy Weiland; Barbara Hunt; Fiona Brennan; Phillip Sanderson; Hatice Abdullah; Gillian Dyson; Dean Brannagan; Helen Sloan; Derek; and to all those who have participated along the way.

INTRODUCTION: CAMERAWALKS
Geoff Cox

T he second book of the Camerawork imprint 'Camerawords' has been playfully renamed 'Camerawalks'. The intention is quite literal: to try to encourage the reader to take a topographic leap of imagination in a re-reading of the 'East End' of London through a play of alliterative signifiers; work, word, walk.

The first book in the '...words' series, *The Impossible Document: Photography and Conceptual Art in Britain, 1966-1976* set itself the serious/arduous task of contributing to the historicisation of conceptual art with a primary focus on photography as an under-theorised concern at that time. It was claimed that as much as photography formed part of a critique of visual culture, it incorporated into the visual mainstream its own representational and institutional limits; perhaps taking up the 'critical realist' challenge of early modernists such as Brecht who famously declared that: "... less than ever does the mere reflection of reality reveal anything about reality. A photograph of the Krupp works or the A.E.G. tells us next to nothing about these institutions. Actual reality has slipped into the functional. The reification of human relations - the factory, say - means that they are no longer explicit. So something must in fact be built up, something artificial, posed.'"[1]

Rather than simply use this familiar quote as a rejection of photography's usefulness as social description as is often the case, or worse to imagine that the social is unknowable through representation, the point is that it is the surface that reveals nothing about these institutions and an alternative has to be 'posed'. Allan Sekula offers an alternative in that if it is the underlying system of exploitation that remains hidden, then it follows that: "Reified social relations are in a sense invisible to ordinary empiricism, and can only be understood through recourse to abstraction, or as Marx put it in the introduction to *Grundrisse*, through the movement upwards

---

1. Brecht, quoted in, Walter Benjamin's "A Small History of Photography" (1931), in, *One Way Street*, London: Verso, 1985, p.255.

from the concrete to the abstract, and back down to the concrete."[2] This exchange between experience and the representation of it leads to the question of how this might be achieved through representation, such that reality might be revealed for what it really is.

Camerawork itself has long been concerned with the employment of photography as a signifying practice and in the early days of its project, considered that documentary practices might offer a challenge to the social order through visibility and a corresponding engagement with a politics of representation. However, the difficulty for photography at this point in time lies in its very incorporation into the mainstream of visual arts practice (not least in the fashionable and nullifying practices of neo-conceptualists) sitting uncomfortably next to its more overt commercial applications. It is all kinds of work, and especially critical work that appears to be occluded in the rush for a post-photographic, post-social imaginary.

The strategy in this '...walks' book is to encourage a close reading/ walking of the urban-city-text, drawing upon a set of other references, disciplines and histories of social description. The allusions here are numerous; from the popular tourist activities of 'London Walks' to the well-trodden academic interest in the 'walking methodologist' (see *A Walk on the East Side*, herein p.21). One widespread vehicle for reading the surface of the city can be found in Baudelaire's 'flâneur' figure strolling along the streets of C19th Paris. Baudelaire saw the wandering in the streets as a method of productive labour of the writer "... stumbling over words like cobblestones, colliding at times with lines I dreamed of long ago". In turn, Benjamin's interest in the flâneur was as a 'figure' for the modern intellectual not expressed as a lofty academic in his/her disconnected study but through walking the streets amongst the crowds in close contact with the object of inquiry. In this upwards and downwards movement, even the most insignificant representations of reality might reveal secret messages in the 'illumination' of detail, suggesting:

"... the meaning of the hidden configuration... it is the phantom

---

2. Allan Sekula, *On 'Fish Story': The Coffin Learns to Dance*, (unpublished notes); see, *Fish Story*, Düsseldorf: Richter Verlag, 1985.

crowd of the words, the fragments, the beginnings of lines from which the poet, in the deserted streets, wrests the poetic booty." In his essay "Das Paris des Second Empire bei Baudelaire" (1938), Benjamin imagines the flâneur at work 'loitering' on the streets, pressing notebooks against the walls as if a desk. The Situationists later reincarnated this strolling figure as 'dérive' literally drifting as a means of reading/reporting on the surface of the modern city. It is as if each person as they proceed through urban space make their own maps as cartographers of a more or less colonial imagination. The suggestion, following Surrealism, was that playful-constructive actions using random chance elements and an awareness of the effects and behaviour induced by psycho-geographical environment would reveal meaning through the very artificiality of urban society. For instance, at the time of the Algerian War, they produced a map of Paris with place names changed for Algerian towns in an ironic reversal of colonial spatial logic.

Such approaches are perhaps in contradistinction to that of Jack London in *The People of the Abyss* of 1903, where he worked 'undercover' in the East End of London to examine the contradiction that at the heart of the immensely wealthy British Empire, there was intense poverty. As much as this was a work of literature, this was also a work of reportage, as he immersed himself in destitution so that he could faithfully record social conditions. Although not referring to London, the place or writer, inadvertently the writer was perhaps operating like a "flâneur-become-detective on the beat... posing as a reporter of the true conditions of urban life, he in fact diverts his audience from its tedium."[3]

For Buck-Morss (clearly expressed in the title of another essay "The Flâneur, the Sandwichman and the Whore: the Politics of Loitering"), we are all flâneur-prostitutes (streetwalkers) in modern consumer society, selling ourselves like commodities to strangers. She continues on the same page, that it is as if the flâneur "takes the concept of being-for-sale itself for a walk"; walking and thinking like a reporter or photojournalist on the conditions of consumer capitalism. Similarly, George Orwell, in *Down and Out in Paris and London* describes the work of Street Photographers, "[who]... have a cunning dodge to stimulate trade. When they see a likely victim

3. Susan Buck-Morss, *The Dialectics of Seeing*, Cambridge, Mass.: M.I.T. Press, 1985, p.306.

approaching, one of them runs behind the camera and pretends to take a photograph. Then, as the victim reaches them, they exclaim: 'There y'are, sir, took yer photo lovely. That'll be a bob.' 'But I never asked you to take it,' protests the victim. 'What, you didn't want it took? Why, we thought you signalled with your 'and. Well, there's a plate wasted! that's cost us sixpence, that 'as.' At this the victim usually takes pity and says he will have the photo after all. The photographers examine the plate and say that it is spoiled, and that they will take a fresh one free of charge. Of course, they have not really taken the first photo; and so, if the victim refuses, they waste nothing."[4]

It is this contradictory connection with the commodity form, and an urban readership of newspaper journalism, that Benjamin anticipates; the 'distracted' channel-hopping of contemporary television viewing, globe-trotting tourism, and surfing the internet as the 'cyber-flâneur'. This is the familiar and fairly negative description of 'lived experience' under consumer capitalism that remains 'hidden' behind the opaque interfaces/screens of the buildings, and anonymous faces in the crowd.

There is certainly a long history of mapping this particular area of London that offers a rich layering of social history and territorial mythology; from the Kray twins to the *Eastenders* soap opera to Iain Sinclair's notion of walking in/out of photographs. Visual artists too have long since bought into this ethnographic fantasy; what might be called the 'themepark' approach of site-specific work.

The walks presented here draw upon these traditions and ideas, but offer the reader a set of instructions, a map of historical references to discover/uncover the changing urban text. The starting point was venue development work in 'Live Arts', funded by the Combined Arts department of the London Arts Board, that facilitated a residency by Tim Brennan during 1996-97. Over a number of years he had been developing a practice which he refers to as 'discursive performance', an approach that offers readings through the structure of a 'guided walk'. The residency itself managed to combine the programming of video screenings of artists who have subjected their

---

4. George Orwell, *Down and Out in Paris and London*, 1933.

bodies to extreme pain and manipulation such as Stuart Brisley and Carolee Schneemann, with a new guided walk entitled *A Cut* designed to link related issues to the exhibition *Orlan: This Is My Body... This Is My Software* (Camerawork, 17 January - 22 February 1997). The walk itself draws upon the richly gory, medical, criminal and political histories of the East End but in a way that de-emphasises or de-centres the body of the performer in favour of the social body. It incorporates the potential for participation of the audience to affect the work through a 'guided' reading of the texts. Under the conditions of the de-materialised artwork extended to the useless body of the artist, it is as if the only viable/tenable action left to the artist is that of a 'guide'.

Such a procedure avoids 'closure' in celebrating the unstable, fluid and transformative qualities of the urban environment through human presence. In this connection, Tim Brennan has cited *Stalker*: "The Zone's a very complex maze of traps. All of them are death traps. I don't know what happens here in the absence of humans but as soon as humans appear, everything begins to move."[5] This type of 'manoeuvring' through urban space rejects the cold distinction between subject and object, observer and observed of orthodox sociology for a phenomenological approach (see *Discursive/ Excursive*, herein p.53). As Heidegger puts it in "The Origins of the Work of Art" in terms that echo the idea of moving from the concrete to the abstract and back again: "In order to hear a bare sound we have to listen away from things, divert our ear from them, ie. listen abstractly."[6] Certainly considerable attention and sensitivity is needed to produce a simultaneous cultural mapping and historical narrating of the East End 'other'. Hal Foster in the essay "The Artist as Ethnographer" calls for reflexivity that "attempts to frame the framer as he or she frames the other."[7] Put another way, this might be a license to write the performing and reading subject into the interface between social structure and social action.

Hereafter, the reader is offered three walks to follow in a more or

---

5. Tim Brennan cites Tarkovsky's film, *Stalker*, (1979), in *Writing & Making,* conference, University of Plymouth, September 1998.

6. Martin Heidegger, "The Origins of the Work of Art", in, *Basic Writings*, New York, 1977, p.156.

7. Hal Foster, "The Artist as Ethnographer", in, *The Return of the Real*, Cambridge, Mass.: MIT Press, 1996, p.203.

less distracted manner. In *One Way Street*, Benjamin advises that: "Work on good prose has three steps: a musical stage when it is being composed, an architectonic one when it is being built, and a textile one when it is woven."[8] This book's approach aims not to see these stages as consecutive but rather as a simultaneous 'collage' that places emphasis on 'weaving' the fragments and quotes into a concrete form. Moreover, this *Guidebook* is to be activated and actualised by the reader...

8. Walter Benjamin, *One Way Street*, London: Verso, 1985, p.61.

Start:
Shadwell Underground Station. E1. Turn right outside Cable St cxit. Stand on rod oyolo track. Stop.
Focus on traffic lights in the distance.

Wait for red light. Text 1. A few paces ahead. Text 2. Cross Cable St opposite Tower Hamlet Offices. View Spanish Civil War commemorative plaque. Straight ahead. Left onto Library Place. Look through fencing. Text 3. View entire mural.

1 Anna Thomas's Black Bread, Peasant Bread:
3/4 pint hot water
4 tablespoons dark molasses
6oz dark breadcrumbs toasted
2 teaspoons dry yeast
1/4 pint lukewarm water
1 teaspoon sugar
1/2 teaspoon ground ginger
12oz rye flour
2 teaspoons salt
3 tablespoons melted butter
6oz white flour
Glaze: beaten egg yoke
Pour the hot water into a large mixing bowl and dissolve the molasses in it.

2 Add the bread-crumbs and mix. Dissolve the yeast in the lukewarm water. Add sugar and ginger. Stir the yeast mixture and let it stand for 15 minutes. When the breadcrumbs have cooled to lukewarm and the yeast is spongy mix them together and stir in the rye flour. Add salt and melted butter. Spread the white flour on a board. Put the mixture on it.

3 Turn the bowl over it and leave it covered for 15 minutes. Knead it vigorously for 10 minutes. When it is smooth and stiff put it in a greased bowl. Turn it over once. Cover it with a towel and let it rise in a warm place until double the bulk, about 1/2 hours. Turn out onto a lightly floured board and shape into a loaf. Place it on a buttered baking sheet, cover, and let it rise again for about 30 minutes.
Before baking, brush the loaf with beaten egg yoke. Bake for 45 minutes at 400F.

1. Trad. recipe for *Russian Black Bread.* 2. Ibid. 3. Ibid.

4 **Stollen:** 1/2 oz fresh yeast, 1/2 level tsp, caster sugar, 4 fl oz tepid milk, 8 oz strong white flour, 1/4 level tsp salt, 1 oz butter, grated rind of 1 small lemon, 2 oz chopped mixed peel, 2 oz currants, 2 oz sultanas, 1 oz blanched almonds, chopped, 1/2 a beaten egg, icing sugar for dusting.

5 **Diego Rivera (1886-1957):** 'For the first time in the history of art, mural painting made the masses the hero of monumental art...' in 1940 Rivera denounced Stalin as 'the undertaker of the Revolution', the betrayer of Spain; by 1952 he was painting a saintly Uncle Joe with a peace dove on one hand and a Stockholm peace petition in the other... Detroit during the Depression... Edsel Ford got Rivera to paint a mural cycle to celebrate the auto industry...

6 ... the American way of death par excellence - was elevated to symbolism, as though it meant something more than a unk of detroit metal (Ford car) hitting a tree on Long Island.

7 'When I am in my painting I'm not aware of what I'm doing. It is only after a sort of get acquainted period that I see what I have been about. I have no fears about making changes, destroying the image, because the painting has a life of its own. I try to let it come through. It is only when I lose contact with the painting that the result is a mess. Otherwise there is pure harmony, an easy give and take, and the painting comes out well.'

8 **The Hand.** Make a transverse incision across the front of the wrist, and a second across the heads of the metacarpal bones, connect the two by a vertical incision in the middle line, and continue it through the centre of the middle finger. The anterior and posterior annular ligaments, and the palmar fascia should first be dissected.

4. Trad. recipe for *German Sweet Bread.* 5. Robert Hughes *Nothing If Not Critical: Selected Essays on Art & Artists*, Collins/Harvill. 1990, pp.203-206. 6. Ibid. p.218. 7. Herbert Read, *A Concise History of Modern Painting*, Thames & Hudson 1968, reprinted 1986, pp.266-267. 8. C.H. Leonard *The Concise Gray's Anatomy*, Omega Books, 1983, p.15.

Retrace steps turning right onto Cable St. Pass bus stop. Sharp right after Tower Hamlets office onto narrow alley. Straight ahead. Into graveyard. If season permits search for crocuses. Text 9.

9 Matzos: Wheatflour & water.

Per Matzo:

Energy	72.00 kcal
	302.00 kj
Protein	2.3 g
Carbohydrates	16.4 g
(of which sugars)	not detected
Fat	0.09 g
(of which saturates)	0.02 g
Fibre	1.2 g
Sodium	less than 0.01 g

The secret of Matzo is what is left out:
No sugar, no added salt or fat. Ideal for low fat and low sodium diets.

---

9. Ingredients for Jewish *Matzos;* unleavened bread.

14

10 Altar Breads:
17 kilograms of flour
19 litres of water

The above is beaten for 4 minutes slowly and then 6 minutes fast to make a thin batter. It is then baked for 90 seconds on an electric plate under pressure to make a thin wafer. The wafers have to be placed in a moist atmosphere for several hours to dampen them before being cut into the traditional round hosts.

We use a refined wheat flour: a brown flour can also be used but it must be wheat and no other ingredients are added excepts water.

The quantities I have given are fairly large as we use a big multiple baking machine. The plates need to be adjusted slightly at times as the quality of the flour varies and this affects the thickness of the batter.

10. Ingredients and recipe for Catholic *Hosts*.

Search for swastika graffiti in graveyard. Face the church.
Approach rear wall of Church. Search for more graffiti. Text 11.
Text 12. Approach front of church.

12 Chapati:
8 oz wholemeal flour
2 tsp ghee, 1/2 pint water

Sift the flour into a bowl, add the
ghee and gradually mix in the
water to make a soft dough.
Knead the dough for a few
minutes, then set it aside in a
covered bowl for 30 minutes.
Break off small pieces of the
dough and roll them out on a
floured surface to make thin
circles.
Cook on a hot griddle for a few
seconds on one side. Turn and
cook the other side for a few
seconds.
Holding the chapati with tongs,
finish cooking it directly over the
flame until it inflates like a ball.
Flatten, spread with a little ghee
and serve hot.

11 Jean Michel Basquiat
first appeared around
1980 as half of a two-
man street-artist team who left
gnomic graffiti in neat block
letters around lower Manhatten
under the tag SAMO, shorthand
for 'SAME OLD SHIT'

---

11. Robert Hughes, op cit, pp.308-309.
12. Ingredients and recipe for *Chapati*.

13 At least 23 killed as gunman opens fire on praying Palestinians

14 A Jewish gunman today shot dead at least 23 Arabs and wounded scores of others in one of Israel's worst massacres of recent years. Some reports put the death toll as high as 45.

The man, wearing an Israeli army officer's uniform, blasted indiscriminately at Arabs as they prayed at a mosque in the West Bank town of Hebron.

The Killer emptied several magazines of his M-16 assault rifle into the crowd before they attacked him with a fire extinguisher.

By then he was dead, but it was not clear whether he shot himself or was beaten to death by the crowd.

13. Theodore Levite and Valentine Low, *Evening Standard,* London, 25 February, 1994, p.1.
14. Ibid.

15 English Whitebread:

3 lb plain flour
I oz salt
I oz lard
I oz fresh yeast
I tsp sugar
I 1/2 pts warm water
(I part boiling, 2 parts cold)

Mix the flour and salt.
Prepare yeast liquid and add with remaining liquid to flour mixture.
Mix well until the dough leaves bowl cleanly.
Knead thoroughly for 10 minutes.
Place dough in a greased bowl, place bowl in a large oiled polythene bag.
Leave until dough has doubled in size, about I hour in a warm place.
Turn dough onto a lightly floured board, knead for about 5 minutes.
Grease 4 x I lb tins, or shape as desired.
Divide dough into 4 equal pieces.
Knead lightly and place in tins.
Place inside large oiled polythene bags and leave in a warm place until the dough is just rounded over the top of the tins, 20-30 minutes.
Remove polythene bags.
Bake in a pre-heated oven 450F for 30 minutes until golden brown.

16 Leavened Dough:

6 C. flour
1/4 C. sugar
I 1/4 C. warm water
I T. yeast
2 T. shortening

(i). Dissolve sugar in warm water, add yeast. (ii). Let the liquid stand for ten minutes. The yeast will foam into a head and rise to the top. (iii). Sift flour, add shortening and mix together with ingredients prepared in step (i). (iv). Knead dough into a ball. (v). Remove dough from bowl. Add flour or water if necessary. (vi). Knead dough until smooth and elastic. (vii). Place dough in a clean bowl and cover with a damp cloth. (viii). Let dough rise (in a warm place) for 2-4 hours until it has doubled or tripled in bulk.

15. Trad. recipe for *English Whitebread*.
16. Ingredients and recipe for *Chinese Leavened Dough*.

17

Irish Soda Bread:
1 lb plain white flour
2 level tsp
bicarbonate of soda, 2 level
tsp cream of tartar, 1 level
tsp salt, 1-2 oz lard, 1/2 pint
soured milk

Grease and flour a baking
sheet. Sift together the dry
ingredients twice. Rub in the
lard. Mix to a soft dough
with the milk, adding a little
at a time.
Shape into a 7 inch round
and mark into triangles.
Place on the baking sheet.
Bake in the oven at 425F for
about 30 minutes.

17. Trad. recipe for *Irish Soda Bread*.

A WALK ON THE EAST SIDE
Chris Jenks

"The wheels rolled on, and rolled down by the Monument, and by the Tower, and by the Docks; down by Ratcliffe, and by Rotherhithe; down from where accumulated scum of humanity seemed to be washed from higher grounds, like so much moral sewage, and to be pausing until its own weight forced it over the bank and sunk it in the river."[1]

The path through the old East End of London, this time towards the sink and degradation of period Limehouse (focusing on the public house we now know as *The Grapes*), is a familiar device for Dickens in creating a gradient towards the very heart of darkness. Those that he joins he does not hate, just as little affection extends to the pomp, mannerism, linguistic absurdity and skilled avarice that he leaves behind in the form of the West End or, less concretely, the middle-class morality of the polite side of town. The journey is always an inverse procession from pseudo-illumination into the opacity of ignorance, abandon and social exclusion. The ironies that accompany the transport are those of class traitorship and the rendering articulate of the lumpen affect that he seeks out and celebrates in the form of poverty and neglect. Dickens was a navigator, but he sought out the Sargasso Sea, the very 'scum' and 'sewage' that choked the channels of the greatest metropolis in the Western World; the forgotten city of the night, but always the night. Dickens charted the lanes for our philanthropy and reform, and for social mobility and the detonation of the nineteenth century *fin de siecle*. He walked the East End, with a purpose.

What purpose do you seek?

Henry Mayhew; Charles Booth; Arthur Morrison; Jack London; George Gissing; Robert Louis Stevenson; Henry James; W.T. Stead; George Sims; James Greenwood; Dore and Jerrold; Arthur Munby; Andrew Mearns; Octavia Hill; Beatrice Webb; Walter Besant -

---

1. Charles Dickens, *Our Mutual Friend*, 1865, p.21.

Victorian walkers all, with a whole spectrum of motivation from the desire for reform to the vicarious lust for the *schadenfreude* deriving from lowlife shock and violence.

For over two centuries now the East End of London has gradually, but resentfully, given up its secrets to the voracious appetites of the bourgeois sensitivities seeking satisfaction in either utopian or dystopian visions but always, ironically, in the hard, factic reality of a geography that symbolises and embodies a culture of marginality and neglect. The East End of London, a dream or nightmare site for walking, stands also as an exploration of those alleyways and backwaters of consciousness where dark and forbidden realities are both expelled and hidden from the clarity of waking. The walker of the eastern streets paces also through the somnambulist fumbles of he or she who seeks to explore the mind.

But perhaps we stride too far ahead.

Reggie Kray, that strutter and owner of the streets, told us while reminiscing about the criminal geography of the 1950s and 1960s that:

"London being made up of so many areas enabled villains to have what they called their own manor, a manor being another name for an area and in whatever direction one would go, north, south, east or west one would come across or encounter some of the villains I am about to mention."[2]

He then proceeded through a litany of underworld baronies, each centred on a pub, a club or a street, and each jealously guarded by a named 'villain' supported by his own adhesive cohort. Relations between criminals within these areas were, we were informed, regulated by 'respect' and their perimeters were demarcated by 'fear'. These tenuous and complementary devices contrived to sustain both the external patchwork of empires and, internal to each, a semblance of community.

This crude social geography could have been part of the continuously reworked romantic fictions of an ageing long-term

---

2. Reg Kray, *Villains We Have Known*, Leeds: NK Publications, 1993, p.7.

prisoner attempting to provide a structured meaning to his past, and also seeking to dramatize his life's ultimate triviality by likening it to the zonal segregation of the 1920s Chicago gangland that he and his twin were known to emulate. However, the lasting point of Kray's account was its endeavour to recollect underworld characters, all real, and all brought vividly to his mind through tracing their 'manors'. It is as if their personae emerged from the very ground on which they stood. Thus the 'villains' are 'seen', or visually re-collected, through their allotted domicile or naturalized location within the city. So serious was the generalized and tacit recognition of 'claimed space', which he chronicled, that all underworld conflicts and gangfights were described finally in terms of boundary disputes. Beyond this, Kray's brother Ronnie was known to have sought justification for his action in publicly executing George Cornell, on 6th March 1966, on the grounds that it constituted retribution, partly for a series of received insults and challenges but primarily, for Cornell's final audacity in penetrating deep into the Kray's territory. The wrong place at the wrong time, he walked where he should have feared to tread.

"... This phone call tells me that Cornell is drinking at a pub called the Blind Beggar, which is right in the middle of our manor and less than half a mile away from where we were drinking."[3]

Assassination, it would appear, was the appropriate punishment for the invasion of territory. Space mattered that much. Even justice became organized in relation to spatial parameters. Patently there were islands in the streets whose denizens, that is, those specifically engaged in such cultural networks, were enthusiastic to live for and, in many instances, willing to suffer injury and even die for.

To attend analytically to the practice of walking is, in large part, to confront and interrogate the concept of social space and, perhaps more specifically, the 'seen' or 'witnessed' character of space and particularly urban space. Space has to be conceptualized in order to be experienced and understood, our 'sites' are informed by the predisposed character of our 'sight'. 'Space', like 'time', in the modern scientific world, has come to be regarded with a categorical fixity and inviolability. Paradoxically, however, humankind has

3. Ron Kray, *My Story*, London: Sidgwick & Jackson, 1993, p.44.

probably been more innovative while, in equal measure, less theoretic about its understanding and use of space through modernity. Some space is both enticing and terrorizing. Nevertheless social scientists and cultural historians, who we might expect to attend to such issues, have only just begun to dislocate and subsequently enmesh space with time, and also discover alternative geographies. The price to be paid for this relative failure of critical theoreticity is that dominant views and appropriations of space have become taken for granted and have, in turn, enabled routine human organization and governance through the controlled orientation of conduct into cellular forms extending from isolation to strategic grouping. We witness this across all manner of modern institutions: in prisons, factories, schools, and the armed services. We witness this as we walk the streets: I regularly stroll across the borders of Lambeth and Southwark and as I do I drift, willfully but unafraid, from 'nuclear free zone' into a potential nuclear desert. People are spatialized, divided, sub-divided, clustered and, therefore, more readily processed. At a more macro level such processing is prevalent in both the conscious and unconscious planning and layout of cities. This occurs through the obvious devices of local governmental authorities, wards, and parish boundaries, but also in term of the unofficial, but nevertheless real evolution of places into 'ghettos', 'loops', 'downtowns', 'West Ends' and 'East Ends' and 'slums'. Engels picked up on this formal/informal segregation in his critical history of nineteenth century Manchester: "He who visits Manchester simply on business need never see the slums, mainly because the working-class districts and the middle-class districts are quite distinct. This division is due partly to deliberate policy and partly to instinctive and tacit agreement of the two groups."[4]

Analytically we are obliged not just to be informed of spatial patterns but to 'see' the meaning that space has reflexively, for ourselves, and then to understand reciprocally the meaning that it has for others.

One common feature of the four extracts quoted above, is that they reveal alternative cartographies of the city. They represent just some of the many potential, and presumably infinite, versions of how the manifestly shared (or at least explicitly public) streets and buildings

4. Quoted in, W. Henderson, Ed., *Engels: Selected Writings*, Harmondsworth: Penguin, 1967, p.27.

delineate fragmented localities and senses of placement and identity. However, such versions, being parochial, never attain more than a partial meaning structure - each of which is a topic. In one dimension the violent realization of the Kray's 'manor' is no more bizarre than Engels's dichotomous understanding of Victorian Manchester, or, shall we say, Richard Hoggart's invocation of his post-war Hunslett in *The Uses of Literacy* or, indeed, any person's allegiance to their home town or neighbourhood.

Different parts of any city carry different and multiple meanings, although such meanings cluster in the same way that recognisable urban 'areas' take form. The justification for these meanings is not solid, it can be sought in a variety of sources. Initially, perhaps, meanings arise from social history through an excavation of a sense of shared cultural sediment. More than this such meanings also find their auspices in our cultural disposition, for example they may be enshrined within a folklore knowledge of any city's 'safe', 'naughty' and 'dangerous' quarters. Or, more rigorously, such meanings emerge through our practices of methodology and through reflexivity. In this last instance we might, for example, approach the growth of London's Dockland, perspectively, as being either a phenomenon of architectural interest or, perhaps, as a material embodiment of a corrupt political economy.

The walker as cultural critic is not new. The archetype walker of modernity is the '*flâneur*', the metaphoric figure originally brought into being by Baudelaire. The flâneur was the spectator and depicter of modern life, most specifically in relation to contemporary art and the sights of the city. The flâneur moves through space and among the people with a viscosity that both enables and privileges vision.

"An observer is a prince who is everywhere in possession of his incognito."[5]

The flâneur, in crude terms, was never a wholly admirable image perhaps because of its potential hauteur. It was, nevertheless, indisputably invested with a certain gaiety and a strong, implicit, irony by Baudelaire; the latter being an important feature, all too readily dispensed with. We detect, within the original depiction, an

5. Charles Baudelaire, *The Painter of Modern Life and Other Essays*, [trans. J. Mayne], London: Phaidon, 1964, p.9.

inquisitive boulevardier always at home with the urban and always urbane at home. However, the flâneur possesses a power, he walks at will, freely and seemingly without purpose, but simultaneously with an inquisitive wonder and an infinite capacity to absorb the activities of the collective - often formulated as 'the crowd'. Perhaps because of these very unconstrained and yet interested characteristics, subsequent appropriations of the concept, most notably by the cultural critic Walter Benjamin, have contributed to the systematic degradation of the stance.

It is not an original idea to see the flâneur in Baudelaire himself, this was, after all, the position adopted by Walter Benjamin. But this is not as straightforward as it might seem. Are we to look at Baudelaire the dandy, the waster, the addict, the dilettante, the depressive? Or are we, perhaps, to identify the pose with Baudelaire the celebrated poet and innovative literary critic - just where are we to find our model? We should, of course, see the dramatic force that sprung from the relation between these two, seemingly irreconcilable, stereotypes.

Yet still, the flâneur is more complex and more versatile than this. The flâneur is not just Baudelaire, though undoubtedly he strolled the boulevards; it is not a descriptive category of that group of the Parisian bourgeoisie who, like Baudelaire, had the time, provided through material comfort, to walk and watch and gain interest and entertainment from the public spectacle. It is not a status location within the stratification system that enables the pastime of "botanizing on the asphalt" or, indeed, the hobby of "taking the turtle for a walk", to borrow two derogatory phrases from Benjamin. The flâneur, though grounded in everyday life, is an analytic form, a narrative device, an attitude towards knowledge and its social context. It is an image of movement through the social space of modernity. The flâneur is a multi-layered palimpsest that enables us to 'move' from real products of modernity, like commodification and leisured patriarchy, through the practical organization of space and its negotiation by inhabitants of a city, to a critical appreciation of the state of modernity and its erosion into the post-, and onwards to a reflexive understanding of the function, and purpose, of realist as opposed to interpretive theories of knowledge in the appreciation of those previous formations.

The flâneur is no concrete reality, a social phenomenon trapped by the essentialism of a materialist critic. It is an alternative 'vision'. It is a vision bred of modernity but equally adaptive, by virtue of its 'cold' stance, to the fragmentations of late-modernity. The wry and sardonic potential built into the flâneur enables resistance to the commodity form and also penetration into its mode of justification, precisely through its unerring scrutiny. Its disinterested interest burns deep into the assumed necessity of consumption and it consequently demotivates the distinction between 'wants' and 'needs'. We witness a procession from scepticism to sight, the amble from doubt into surety. There is no requirement that the flâneur should be implicated in the appropriation of his subject or the fetishization of that subject into commodity-form for, as the materialist critiques also suggest, the stance just 'takes it or leaves it'! The march of modernity is checked by the Nietzschean dance of the flâneur. In addition, the sedentary mannerism of the flâneur: the 'retracing'; the 'rubbernecking'; and the 'taking a turtle for a walk'; are essentially critical rebuffs to the late-modern politics of speed. This walker is persistently ungainly. Following modernity's stable epoch of historical inevitability, we are now witnessing innovations in the vocabulary of time which drastically alter our relation to the whole set of cultural configurations that were established under modernity's central meta-narrative, namely 'progress'. What better place for the flâneur as cultural critic? Resistance wrought through a change of pace, or walking 'out of step' with the late-modern rhythm of the city.

The flâneur sees and walks, and, as we have shown, is not fearful of his tread. One 'seen' chronology of his labyrinthine route is the journey from Baudelaire through Surrealism to the Situationist International. Such a route expresses an interest that is perpetually fresh, or indeed, infantile in its perceptions. This is an interest undaunted by the uniformity of the consumer culture. The emphasis is on the bizarre, the wholly unexpected, even the mysterious and spell-like occurrences within modernity. Such a decoding of the demonic or alchemic in everyday life rests on no formal methodology but on a 'popular cultur(e)'-al 'street' reading of the sights of the city, the knowledge of the walker. The flâneur experiences downward mobility!

The leading figure in the Situationist International is Guy Debord who provides three central concepts which are wholly relevant to the walking methodologist (the flâneur within the [post]modern city), these being: 'the dérive'; 'détournement'; and, perhaps most significantly, the 'spectacle'.

The 'dérive' is the practice through which 'psycho-geographies'are achieved. The term, literally applied, means 'drifting', however that is insufficient a meaning to exhaust the concept's potential. To simply drift implies a passivity that blows with the wind' whereas the 'dérive' demands a response to inducement, albeit unplanned and unstructured. A 'psychogeography' depends upon the walker 'seeing' and being drawn into events, situations and images by an abandonment to wholly unanticipated attraction. We return to a movement that will not be planned, or organized instrumentally - it will not be mobilized. The stroll of the flâneur in the 'dérive' is not purposefully from A to B, not along the boulevard to 'les Grands Magasins', and not intentionally up and down the Arcades. In the 'dérive' the explorer of the city follows whatever cue, or indeed clue, that the streets offer as enticement to fascination.

A psycho-geography, then, dérives from the subsequent 'mapping' of an unrouted route which, like primitive cartography, reveals not so much randomness and chance as spatial intentionality. It uncovers compulsive currents within the city along with unprescribed boundaries of exclusion and unconstructed gateways of opportunity. The city begins, without fantasy or exaggeration, to take on the characteristics of a map of the mind. The legend of such a mental map highlights projections and repressions in the form of 'go' and 'no-go' space. These positive and negative locational responses claim, in their turn, as deep a symbolic significance in the orientation of space as do the binary moral arbiters of 'purity' and 'danger''or the 'sacred' and the 'profane' in relation to the organization of conduct. Such an understanding propels the flâneur towards an investigation of the exclusions and invitations that the city.

The concept of 'détournement' emerges from modernist avant-garde artistic practice. Simply stated it consists of the re-cycling, re-positioning, or re-employing of the existing elements of an art work, or works, into a new synthesis. The two principles of the practice are: (a) that each re-used element from a previous context must be divested of its autonomy and original signification; and (b) that the re-assembly of elements must forge an original image which generates a wholly new meaning structure for the parts, through the totality that they now comprise. 'Détournement' provides the flâneur with the perceptual tools for spatial irony. The walker in 'dérive', who is therefore not oriented by convention, can playfully and artfully 'see' the juxtaposition of the elements that make up the city in new and revealing relationships. The planned and unplanned segregations, the strategic and accidental adjacencies, and the routine but random triangulations that occur through the mobility that the city provides, and depends upon, make for a perpetual and infinite collage of imagery and a repository of fresh signification. All of this conceptual re-ordering is open to the imaginative theorizing of the wandering urban cultural critic and yet mostly such techniques have come to be the province of the photo-journalist. The image of the city formed by the flâneur should be part of his critical self-awareness; it reveals both modernity and the projections, inhibitions, repressions and prejudices of the flâneur.

Finally, and formative of both of the above ideas, is the concept of 'the spectacle'. The spectacle is that which constitutes the visual convention and fixity of contemporary imagery. It is a reactionary force in that it resists interpretation. It is a prior appropriation of the visual into the form of the acceptably viewable, and this 'acceptability' befits the going order. The spectacle indicates rules of what to see and how to see it, it is the 'seen-ness', the (re)presentational aspect of phenomena that are promoted, not the politics or aesthetics of their being 'see-worthy.' From within this critical concept the flâneur can deduce, and thus claim distance from, the necessity of objects-to-be-seen as appearing in the form of commodities. People and their places; space as an intertextuality of narratives of social life; and the 'sights of the city'; are not objects at hand for the gaze of the consumer, that is, the tourist in the lives of the collective other. This takes us back to the notion that the flâneur should/could not merely mingle with the crowd, but is an interactor and thus a constitutor of the people's crowd-like-ness. Social life is degraded rather than honoured by its transformation into the realm of 'the spectacle'. It is, ironically, the realist reduction at the core of materialist ideas, such as have sought to critique the flâneur, which are more adept at standardizing and routinizing the relation between signifier and signified into the form of a positive 'spectacle'. Peter Ackroyd, the contemporary author of urban fiction, the master of mystical realism, another street walker who claims a vocal relation with history, has stated through one of his characters:

"And it did not take any knowledge of the even more celebrated Whitechapel murders, all of them conducted in the streets and alleys around Christ Church, Spitalfields, to understand, as Hawksmoor did, that *certain streets or patches of ground provoked a malevolence which generally seemed to be quite without motive.*"[6]

The (post)modern flâneur, you, me, we as walkers, can equally well recognise the real, as well as supposed, character of the city's threats, intimidations, menaces or simply challenges to free access. The East End of London may never have been a 'jungle' or 'dark continent' and it may not be accurately delineated along its front line by the Aldgate Pump, Middlesex Street and Norton Folgate but it has, in several senses 'an edge"which is as recognisable to the outsider as it is to the inhabitant. The East End both 'includes' and 'excludes', it is an enclave from the mainstream of city dwelling and is recognised as such by all. I am not referring to just a passive residue bequeathed by history but rather a living tradition.

Let me allow a final word to Iain Sinclair the inveterate, obsessional East End walker and decoder of the complex ciphers of the old town, the translator of the obscure urban tongue. Caught up in the bizarre and frenetic circus that swept in the vortex of Ronnie Krays' funeral procession he notes:

"Expectant crowds had gathered early, blue jeans and brown leather jackets set against the long coats of the minders, the jewellery, coiffures and dark glasses, of the public mourners, local celebrities recognised only by their own. I decided to take Marc with me and follow the procession on foot. The concept of 'strolling', aimless urban wandering, the flâneur had been superseded. We had moved into an age of the stalker; journeys made with intent - sharp-eyed

---

6. Peter Ackroyd, *Hawksmoor*, London: Hamish Hamilton, 1985, p.116.

and unsponsored. The stalker was our role model: purposed hiking, not dawdling, nor browsing. No time for savouring of reflections in shop windows, admiration for Art Nouveau ironwork, attractive matchboxes rescued from the gutter. This was walking with a thesis. With a prey."[7]

---

7. Iain Sinclair, *Lights Out For the Territory*, London: Granta Books, 1997, p.75.

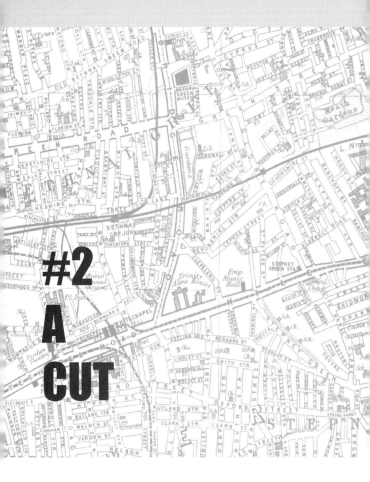

#2
A
CUT

Newark St. E1. Facing commemorative brown plaque to John Richard Green. Read plaque. Text 1.

1 The aim of the following work is defined by its title; it is a history, not of English Conquests, but of the English People.... At the risk of sacrificing much that was interesting and attractive in itself, and which the constant usage of our historians has made familiar to English readers, I have preferred to pass lightly and briefly over the details of foreign wars and diplomacies, the personal adventures of kings and nobles, the pomp of courts, or the intrigues of favourites, and to dwell at length on the incidents of that constitutional, intellectual, and social advance in which we read the history of the nation itself. It is with this purpose that I have devoted more space to Chaucer than to Cressy, to Caxton than to the petty strife of Yorkist and Lancastrian, to the Poor Law of Elizabeth than to the Young Pretender.

LCC

JOHN
RICHARD GREEN
Historian of the
English People
Lived here
1866-1869

JOHN RICHARD GREEN
AUTHOR OF THIS WORK
WAS THE INCUMBENT
OF ST. PHILIP'S CHURCH
NEWARK STREET, E.1.
1866 - 1869

1. John Richard Green, *Short History of the English People*, London, 1892, p.xxiv.

Cross Newark St. to entrance to Royal London Hospital Archives.
Proceed part way down ramp.
Text 2.

2 That was the end of his story. Both the story-teller and the tale he told excited the whole company, but Theseus most of all. As he was clamouring to hear more of the wonderful deeds of the gods, the river god of Calydon raised himself on his elbow, and addressed the hero in these words: 'There are some, bravest Theseus, whose shape has been changed just once, and has then remained permanently altered. Others again have power to change into several forms. Take for instance, Proteus, the god who dwells in the sea that encircles the earth. People have seen him at one time in the shape of a young man, at another transformed into a lion; he used to appear to them as a raging wild boar, or again as a snake which they shrank from touching; or else horns transformed him into a bull. Often he could be seen as a stone, or a tree, sometimes he presented the appearance of running water, and became a river, sometimes he was the very opposite, when he turned into fire.

2. Ovid, *Metamorphoses*, Book VIII, translated by Mary M. Innes, Penguin, 1955, p.198.

Enter archives. View contents on display. Ask at desk to view video: _Open Wide. Cutting Edge._ (Yorkshire TV, 1994). Text 3. Leave the building. Proceed part way up ramp.

3 Joseph Merrick, the 19th century Englishman who was called the Elephant Man because of his grotesque appearance, did not suffer from the disease that is named after him, say radiologists in London.

X-ray and CT scans of Merrick's remains suggest that he did not have neurofibromatosis, a disfiguring condition sometimes called Elephant Man disease. Anita Sharma and her colleagues at The Royal London Hospital gave their diagnosis earlier this week at the annual meeting of the Radiological Society of North America in Chicago. The radiologists say that the strongest evidence yet that Merrick suffered from a much rarer disease called Proteus syndrome.

Neurofibromatosis is a genetic disorder that causes uncontrolled growth of nerve cells, so people develop unsightly tumours beneath the skin. Patients often undergo repeated surgery to remove the tumours beneath the skin. Proteus syndrome involves the abnormal growth of bone and soft tissue. Like neurofibromatosis, it is thought to be a genetic disease. There have been fewer than 100 recorded cases.

Merrick died in 1890 at the London Hospital, where he had lived for four years after being rescued from a life as a circus freak by the doctor Frederick Treves. Merrick's remains were kept at the hospital, which is now called the Royal London.

Sharma says that his skeleton shows the telltale signs of Proteus syndrome and lacks characteristics that would be expected of someone with neurofibromatosis. Merrick's skeleton is studded with bony outgrowths, predominantly on the right-hand side. His ring finger and femur are both enlarged, and his skull has a circumference of 91 centimetres, compared to the 60 centimetres typical for a man of his height.

Neurofibromatosis patients usually have sharply curved spines, but Merrick's spine has a much shallower curvature. His ribs also lack notches common in neurofibromatosis, and are abnormally thickened. People with neurofibromatosis usually have thinner ribs than normal.

In recent years, Proteus syndrome has been gathering support as the favoured diagnosis for Merrick. In 1987, a panel commissioned by the US National Institutes of Health to assess research in neurofibromatosis concluded that Merrick was probably disfigured by the rare syndrome, rather than Elephant Man disease.

Merrick's autopsy records and tissue samples taken at the time of his death were lost during the Second World War. In future, geneticists may remove fragments of bone from Merrick's skeleton and conduct DNA tests to see if his cells carry the gene for neurofibromatosis, which American geneticists isolated on chromosome 17 in 1990. "Only then will we know for sure," says Sharma.

---

3. Vincent Kiernan, _New Scientist_, 7 December 1996, p.12.

Through gates. Turn left onto Newark St. Straight ahead. First left into pedestrian area. Straight ahead. Turn right onto Stepney Way. Straight ahead. Second left to rear of Hospital and down a ramp which arrives at a basement. View the former entrance to Merrick's home which is now a bricked up. Text 4.

4 There is a bay in Haemonia, curved like a sickle, and enclosed by jutting arms, where there would be a harbour, if the water were deeper: but the waves just cover the surface of the sand. It has a firm shore, free from seaweed, where the sand retains no footprints and yet does not clog one's steps.

I am an oddity at fairs
They pay to gaze
In gawping horror
Focus of stairs
Each thanking God
My body is not theirs.

God? Does one exist,
That He should fashion
One like me? I am His joke;
The mis-shaped clay
The careless potter tossed aside,
Who only in perfection takes a pride.

My forehead overhangs
Like some great cliff,
A nose that's but
A mound of flesh;
Whilst from my mouth
Protrudes a fungoid growth.

From chest and back
Hangs cauliflower skin,
That has a smell. I have
One perfect arm, one gross,
And I am lame as well.

Yet, dragging this vile body
Round the years,
I am not what
At first appears,
A senseless freak,
Devoid of hope or tears.

When he had said this, Proteus submerged his head in the sea, letting the waters close over his final words.

4. Ovid, *Metamorphoses*, Book XI, Penguin, 1955, p.252; Poem allegedly written by Joseph Merrick, Education File, Royal London Hospital Archives; Ovid, op.cit. p.253.

5 Catherine Moreton. Aged 22, has a B.A. (Hons.) French with Subsidiary Italian. My father suggested I should become a nurse. He said it would help me to help others, and he is right. The job makes me feel very happy and some evenings I am really amazed to have passed such a happy day amongst people who are suffering. I can only hope that my happiness has given the patients some too.

Each day brings its own reward. If you have managed to make a patient confortable - and he often tells you-you have all the reward you want. In a few months I shall be married, but I shall continue nursing as it is so rewarding. Nursing not only gives me the confidence to help other people but to make happy, close relationships in my own life. Hours of nursing, even full time, are in many hospitals very convenient to the married woman. Early duty, even if it is really early, at least allows you to be home before your husband. No doubt once I have qualified I will have a family, but there is only one job I would ever like to return to - nursing.

6 As for the loathsome Propoetides, they dared to deny the divinity of Venus. The story goes that as a result of this, they were visited by the wrath of the goddess, and were the first women to lose thair good names by prostituting themselves in public. Then, as all sense of shame left them, the blood hardened in their cheeks, and it required only a slight alteration to transform them into stony flints.

When Pygmalion saw these women, living such wicked lives, he was revolted by the many faults which nature has implanted in the female sex, and long lived a bachelor existence, without any wife to share his home. But meanwhile, with marvelous artistry, he skilfully carved a snowy ivory statue. He made it lovelier than any woman born, and fell in love with his own creation. The statue had all the appearance of a real girl, so that it seemed to be alive, to want to move, did not modesty forbid. So cleverly did his art conceal its art. Pygmalion gazed in wonder, and in his heart there rose a passionate love for this image of a human form. Often he ran his hands over the work, feeling it to see whether it was flesh or ivory, and would not yet admit that ivory was all it was. He kissed the statue, and imagined that it kissed him back, spoke to it and embraced it, and thought he felt his fingers sink into the limbs he touched, so that he was afraid lest a bruise appear where he had pressed the flesh. Sometimes he addressed it in flattering speeches, sometimes brought the kind of presents that girls enjoy: shells and polished pebbles, little birds and flowers of a thousand hues, lilies and painted balls, and drops of amber which fall from the trees that were once Phaethon's sisters. He dressed the limbs of his statue in woman's robes, and put rings on its fingers, long necklaces round its neck. Pearls hung from its ears, and chains were looped upon its breast. All this finery became the image well, but it was no less lovely unadorned. Pygmalion then placed the statue on a couch that was covered with cloths of Tyrian purple, laid its head to rest on soft pillows, as if it could appreciate them, and called it his bedfellow.

5. Jane Moreton, "Nurses Viewpoint", in *Hospital Career,* Vol. 4, no.1. Sept. 1972, p.14.
6. Ovid, *Metamorphoses,* Book X, Penguin, 1955, p.231.

7 The police closed down the exhibition forcing the showman to take Merrick to the continent. In Brussels, in 1886 the exhibition was banned again and the showman sent Merrick back to London alone. Upon arrival at Liverpool Street Station, the police had to rescue him from an excitable crowd. An appeal letter to The Times newspaper successfully raised funds enabling him to remain as a resident of the London Hospital and two rooms were converted into a flat for him. He died in bed aged 27 either from suffocation or dislocation of his neck due to his heavy skull falling backwards.

a cut ....

In 1986 259 Whitechapel Rd was the premises of D.J. SMITH – Butcher

In 1886 259 Whitechapel Rd was 124/125 Whitechapel Rd belonged to George Roberts – pawn broker.

In 1884 he was exhibited as 'The Elephant Man' in a vacant shop outside

7. "Biography and Clinical History", Education File, Royal London Hospital Archives.

[618-283]

Turn right. Straight ahead. First left onto Brady St. Straight ahead. Stop at corner of Durwood St.
Text 8.

8 'The festival of Venus, which is celebrated with the greatest pomp all through Cyprus, was now in progress, and heifers, their crooked horns gilded for the occasion, had fallen at the altar as the axe struck their snowy necks. Smoke was rising from the incense, when Pygmalion, having made his offering, stood by the altar and timidly prayed, saying: 'If you gods can give all things, may I have as my wife, I pray -' he did not dare say 'the Ivory maiden,' but finished: 'one like the ivory maid.' However, golden Venus, present at her festival in person, understood what his prayers meant, and as a sign of that the gods were kindly disposed, the flames burned up three times, shooting a tongue of fire into the air. When Pygmalion returned home, he made straight for the statue of the girl he loved, leaned over the couch, and kissed her. She seemed warmed: he laid his lips on hers again, and touched her breast with his hands - at his touch the ivory lost its hardness, and grew soft: his fingers made an imprint on the yielding surface, just as wax of Hymettus melts in the sun and, worked by men's fingers, is fashioned into many different shapes, and made fit for use by being used. The lover stood, amazed, afraid of being mistaken, his joy tempered with doubt, and again and again stroked the object of his prayers. It was indeed a human body! The veins throbbed as he pressed them with his thumb. Then Pygmalion of Paphos was eloquent in his thanks to Venus. At long last, he pressed his lips upon living lips, and the girl felt the kisses he gave her, and blushed. Timidly raising her eyes, she saw her lover and the light of day together. The godess Venus was present at the marriage she had arranged and, when the moon's horns had nine times been rounded into a full circle, Pygmalion's bride bore a child, Paphos, from whom the island takes its name.

8. Ovid, *Metamorphoses*, Book X, Penguin, 1955, p.232.

39

Turn left down Durwood St. Stop on left just before the street opens out into a small bus station. View the ground on the left near the wall to the former Victorian school buildings. Text 9.

9 Friday, August 31st: Mary Anne Nicholls, aged 42, known as Polly. Her body was found in Bucks Row (now Durward Street) by a carter on his way to work at 3.20 a.m. Her throat had been cut. A doctor examining her body did not examine the injuries beneath her clothes.

9. Alexander Kelly with David Sharp, *Jack The Ripper*, A.A.L., 1995, p.8.

10 P.C.97 J. Neil reports at 3.45 a.m., 31st inst. [August], he found the dead body of a woman lying on her back with her clothes a little above her knees, with her throat cut from ear to ear on a yard crossing at Bucks Row, Whitechapel. P.C. obtained the assistance of P.C.'s 55 H.Mizen and 96 J. Thain. The latter called Dr. Llewellyn, No.152 Whitechapel Rd. He arrived quickly and pronounced life to be extinct, apparently but a few minutes. He directed her removal to the Mortuary, stating he would make a further examination there, which was done on the ambulance.

11 Gerry Lewis. Male Nurse Aged 21. Nursing as far as I am concerned is not the soft occupation that most men would consider it to be. First of all, it is interesting, you deal with people and you have to be a match for many a difficult situation. There is a lot to learn and the balance of this learning may at some time decide the difference between life and death. If you are not willing to accept hard work and a certain amont of responsibility then you can forget all about nursing.

Although working with so many women can be trying, especially when in the minority yourself, it does have its compensations. At the beginning of my training I was apprehensive as to how I would get along with twenty seven girls in my study block. After the first intial weeks of settling in I was accepted by the girls as a member of the group. I feel that if more men could get over the initial difficulties of training with so many girls then more of them would take up the profession. As it is I see an ever growing demand for male nurses.

Before nursing I spent two years at technical college taking 'A' Levels. I found time to travel to the Far East and I did a variety of jobs including barman and pipe laying. I came into nursing because I was looking for a career that was both rewarding and interesting and one that also offered good prospects for the future. I think that I have found what I was looking for in nursing.

10. Stephen Knight, *Jack the Ripper - The Final Solution*, Harrap, 1976, pp.49-50.
11. Gerry Lewis, "Nurses Viewpoint", in, *Hospital Career*, Vol. 4, no.1, Sept. 1972, p.15.

Turn right onto Vallance Rd. Straight ahead. Stop next to waste ground. Texts 12 & 13. Continue along Vallance Rd. Sharp right across grassed area. Pass derelict Metropolitan drinking fountain on right. Continue across grass to the rear of flats. Enter the square which is located in the estate. View plaque commemorating the last V2 bomb-site of WW2. Straight ahead.

12 Whitechapel had no mortuary. Bodies were taken to a shed next to the workhouse. The body of Mary Ann ('Polly') Nicholls was examined haphazardly being stripped in the shed by 2 workhouse inmates without permission or authority. One of them, Hatfield was asked;

What did you take off first?

An ulster, which I put side on the ground. We then took the jacket off, and put it in the same place . The outside dress was loose, and we did not cut it. The bands of the petticoats were cut, and then I tore the chemise down the front. There were no stays.

The 'Mortuary Keeper' was prone to fits.

13 The Ripper had made several deep cuts in the woman's abdomen, but no organs were actually missing. The murder had taken place between 2.30 a.m., when Polly Nicholls was last seen alive, and 3.15, and the killer had worked silently and quickly - a woman in a bedroom above the murder scene heard nothing.

12. From the inquest transcript of Mary Anne Nicholls, Bancroft Library Archives, London.
13. Alexander Kelly & David Sharp, op.cit. p.8.

Enter the pub on Selby St. Buy a drink. Search for porcelain ornament in the style of Boticelli's Venus. Ask the proprietor to switch the ornament's light on. Exit pub. Cross Selby Straight and proceed up Hemmings St. Search in the gutter for surgical gloves. Straight ahead. Stop underneath the railway bridge. Text 14.

14

Reg Kray. Life Prisoner. There is no cultural life in prison, other than that of one's own making. Most of mine stems from the radio which I listen to in the early hours, usually Melody FM because it plays all the music I love, romantic ballads mostly. In the evenings I often tune in to Caesar the Geezer on Capital Gold - a phone-in with music. I consider Caesar to be a man of principle and his programme is very much alive. It keeps me in touch with the outside world.

My favourite singers are the great Frank Sinatra, the voice of all time, Al Jolson and Elton John. I like East 17 - Brian Harvey has a great voice. The songs I relate to are 'The Power of Love' by Jennifer Rush, 'Strangers In The Night' (which reminds me of Tangiers - my favourite place), 'No Regrets' and 'Imagine' by John Lennon. I visualise one day there will be a world, one nation, no religion, just as the song says. I do not believe in religion, although I do believe in God and Jesus. Television doesn't interest me. I don't like sitting in a room with strangers watching other people's lives. I prefer to experience life in the flesh.

Theatre used to be my favourite pastime. I had the pleasure of seeing 'Oh What A Lovely War!' by the brilliant playwright Joan Littlewood. La Scala Theatre in Milan also holds fond memories for me. I watched 'Madam Butterfly' there with my late wife Frances. Covent Garden also gave me great relaxation. I met Joan Sutherland backstage there, and presented her with a bouquet and a kiss. It was a night of acclaim for the lady. I've read many books and I prefer fact to fiction. I enjoyed Brendan Behan's 'Borstal Boy' which I thought was very true to life. Kahlil Gibran's 'The Prophet' is a favourite; it has profound thoughts. 'Bury My Heart At Wounded Knee' by Dee Brown left me full of great sorrow. 'Wisdom Of The Ages' is another interesting book - it's full of beautiful proverbs involving every aspect of life. Proverbs say a lot in a few words. I've written one of my own which is: More often than not the written word is truth. These books have inspired me to write, and so far I've had five books published. My philosophy is to live for the moment and I count my blessings. Catch the moment, it is as elusive as a butterfly, gone in the blinking of an eyelid.

14. Reg Kray, "My Cultural Life", interview with Caroline Egan, *The Guardian*, 17 January, 1997, p.3.

Straight ahead. Turn right onto Dunbridge St. Straight ahead.
Railway line on right. Dunbridge St. becomes Three Colts Lane.
Text 15.

15 Al Luoi Chon, Aged 19. I am a girl who comes 10,000 miles
from Malaysia. There are lots of other girls who have either
come to England to take up nursing or to go to University...
I decided to come to England to learn nursing as I find it is a very
interesting and worthwhile job, where I can make many friends and
learn much about the English way of life and people. I also like
travelling and to come to England was a wonderful experience...
Ever since I was in lower secondary school nursing has interested me.
The sight and people dying around me made me very determined to
try and help them in their misery...
All the other girls are very friendly.

15. Al Luoi Chon, "Nurses Viewpoint", in, *Hospital Career*, Vol. 4, no.1., Sept. 1972, p.14.

Stop at the corner of Wilmot St at the foundation stone to the former Good Shepherd Ragged School. Text 16.

16 The Cripples Band (in connection with the Shaftsbury Society). This excellent work has grown under the superintendance of Mr. W.Rawles and Mrs. Ruddell. Between 50 and 60 cripples are now on the list, all of whom have been visited from time to time. Those able to leave their home have also enjoyed entertainments given at this School (where Mr. and Mrs. J.W. Richardson delighted them with sketches in coloured chalks, to a musical accompaniment), at the People's Palace, at the LycettMemorial Chapel, and elsewhere; and in the summer they were conveyed to the Shaftsbury Retreat at Loughton. A number of them received Christmas hampers, and many took advantage of the system of exchanging interesting books for home reading. There is a special class for cripples in the afternoon school.

The Band of Hope... after sinking somewhat low, has shown renewed vitality. At the end of the year it contained 97 children, all pledged to abstain from intoxicating drink. The meetings are held on Wednesday evening, from 7.15 until 8.15.

16. "43rd Annual Report", The Good Shepherd & Abbey Street Sunday & Ragged Schools, Wilmot Street, Bethnal Green Road, March 14, 1899, The Bancroft Library Archives, London.

Proceed along Three Colts Lane. Third left onto Coventry Rd. Straight ahead. Second Right onto Witan St. First left onto Cambridge Heath Rd. Straight ahead. Cross road to entrance gates to park. Text 16. Enter park. Straight ahead. Stop at the right hand side of Bethnal Green Public Library. Search for graffiti: 'I Love Drugs'. Text 17.

17 ...'several of the pauper women were chained to their bedsteads naked, and only covered with an hempen rug' (that was in December)... that the patients were subjected to brutal cruelties from attendants; that they suffered very much from cold (one patient having lost her toes from mortification, proceeding from cold) and that they were infested with vermin.

17. "Bethnal Green Pauper Lunatic Asylum Report of the Commissioners: 1848" in A.T. Robinson & D.H.B. Cheshyre, *A History of the Heart of Bethnal Green* , Bancroft Library Archives, London. p.14.

18 On August 13 Trelawny placed on the Bolivar a sheet-iron furnace, fuel, and spices, and proceeded to the spot where Williams's body was buried. There he was met by a military guard, to assist him and also to see that the cremation did not violate the quarantine laws. Everything was made ready, and Byron and Hunt were notified to be present next morning. They drove out from Pisa and were joined by a Tuscan military guard. Wood was collected and piled up, the body was exhumed and placed in its iron box, the torch was applied, and for some time the fire burned furiously. As soon as they could approach the furnace, Williams's friends threw frankincense, salt, wine, and oil upon the body. By four o'clock in the afternoon (Byron and Trelawny having meanwhile taken a swim) the body had been reduced to ashes. The furnace was cooled in the sea, and Williams's ashes were placed in an oak box and given to Byron, who was to take them to Pisa, whence they were to accompany Jane Williams to England.

---

18. Newman Ivey White *Shelley* , Vol. 2., Secker & Warburg, 1947, p.381.

Straight ahead. Text 19. Second left onto Globe Rd. Cross Rd.
First right onto Digby St. Straight ahead. Stop at enclosed
children's play area on left.

19 Next day the same ceremony was repeated with Shelley's
body. As the diggers sought for the body Trelawny stood aside
and thought what a desecration he was committing by this
last necessary act of service to his friend. Why not leave him here with
the sea in front and the wooded mountains behind him, in the midst
of the solitude and natural grandeur that had given him so much
pleasure? Byron stood silent and thoughtful; Leigh Hunt had remained
in the carriage, alone with his reflections... A dull thud announced the
location of the body. The ceremony of the previous day was repeated.
Heat-waves from the fire and the sun made the air visible and
tremulous; the quick-lime, the oil, and the salt made vari-coloured
flames above the corpse. The iron box was now white-hot and the
contents were slowly turning to grey ashes. A few bits of bone
remained unconsumed, and, strangely, the heart also. Of the English
party only Trelawny had fortitude enough to face this final scene. It
would appear that the military officer also turned away, for Trelawny
found an opportunity to rescue Shelley's heart, unobserved, though
he burned his hand in doing so. The ashes were placed in a box and
carried on board the Bolivar, and the spectators and participants
went their various ways.

L LUOI CHON, Aged 19.

am a girl who comes 10,000 miles f
There are lots of other girls who l

19. Ibid. p.382.

Search for commemorative plaque to Sidney Frank Godley VC. Proceed along Digby St. First left onto Bacton St. Stop at barrier. Text 20.

CHAPTER

5

20 **It was on a dreary night of November that I beheld the accomplishment of my toils. With an anxiety that almost amounted to agony, I collected the instruments of life around me, that I might infuse a spark of being into the lifeless thing that lay at my feet. It was already one in the morning; the rain pattered dismally against the panes, and my candle was nearly burnt out, when, by the glimmer of the half-extinguished light, I saw the dull yellow eye of the creature open; it breathed hard, and a convulsive motion agitated its limbs.**

How can I describe my emotions at this catastrophe, or how delineate the wretch whom with such infinite pains and care I had endeavoured to form? His limbs were in proportion, and I had selected his features as beautiful. Beautiful! Great God! His yellow skin scarcely covered the work of muscles and arteries beneath; his hair was of a lustrous black, and flowing; his teeth of pearly whiteness; but these luxuriances only formed a more horrid contrast with his watery eyes, that seemed almost of the same colour as the dun-white sockets in which they were set, his shrivelled complexion and straight black lips.

The different accidents of life are not so changeable as the feelings of human nature. I had worked hard for nearly two years, for the sole purpose of infusing life into an inanimate body. For this I had deprived myself of rest and health. I had desired it with an ardour that far exceeded moderation; but now that I had finished, the beauty of the dream vanished, and breathless horror and disgust

20. Mary Shelley, *Frankenstein*, first published 1818, republished Penguin, 1994, p.55.

21 'Then I led her to the pole', he continues, 'to which she was lightly bound, and a bandage tied over her eyes which, as the soldier who put it on told me later, were full of tears. A few seconds now passed which appeared like an eternity because the Catholic priest spoke longer with M. Baucq. Then one sharp command was given, two salvoes rang out at the same moment from two parties of eight men at six paces, and both the condemned sank to the ground without a sound. My eyes were fixed exclusively on Miss Cavell, and what I saw was terrible. With a face streaming with blood - one shot had gone through her forehead - she had sunk down forward, but three times seemed to raise herself up without a sound. I ran forward with the medical man but he was right when he stated these were merely reflex movements as bullet holes, as large as a fist in her back, proved that she was killed imediately. The doctor certified death and a few minutes later two plain wooden coffins were lowered into graves.'

21. A.E. Clark Kennedy, *Edith Cavell: Pioneer & Patriot*, Faber & Faber, 1965, p.224.

✱ i) "Discursive": (from Latin: *discurrere*: to run hither and thither), *The Shorter Oxford English Dictionary* gives: "2. Passing rapidly or irregularly from subject to subject; rambling, digressive; ranging over many subjects". More recently the word has taken over the meanings formerly held by "discursory', viz. "of the nature of discourse' and it is in this sense that it is used in 'Discourse Analysis within Linguistic Pragmatics' (cf, Gillian Brown & George Yule, *Discourse Analysis*, Cambridge 1983) which studies language units above the level of the sentence, and in the socio-epistemological work of Michel Foucault on 'discursive formations' cf: *The Archaeology of Knowledge* (1969) trans., A.M. Sheridan Smith (London 1973). For a useful survey of this field, see Diane Macdonell, *Theories of Discourse, an Introduction* (Oxford, 1986). The account of Tim Brennan's practice in this chapter burrows behind the level of ideological description so as to locate those fundamental and inescapable existential structures that constitute the conditions for discursive formations. In my understanding this pays attention to the process of the work while fully engaging the range of discursive practice it may enable, without foreclosing hermeneutic possibilities disclosed by the work. The work of Martin Heidegger, in its deconstruction ('destruktion', cf: "destructuring - which is to be understood literally as a deconstruction or painstaking dismantling," from, David Farrell Krell's note in his ed., *Martin Heidegger, Basic Writings* (London 1978, 2nd ed. 1994 p.39) of Cartesian subject-object dualism (*Being and Time*, sections pp.19-24), gives some means of approach to this level. Foucault made his debt to Heidegger very explicit in his last interviews, describing him as an 'overwhelming influence', who had determined his 'entire philosophical development' (see Michel Foucault, 'Truth, Power, Self; an interview with Michel Foucault' in *Technologies of Self: Seminar with Michel Foucault*, ed L.H. Martin, H. Gutman, & P.H.Hutton, (Amherst 1988 p.12-13), and 'The Return of Morality', in *Politics, Philosophy, Culture: Interview and other Writings 1977-1984* ed. Lawrence D Kritzman (London, 1988 p.243). In summary, if these excursions are, by the same token, discursive performances, a phenomenological analysis of their process should lay bare a network of discursive possibilities through which, in performance, the participants are enabled to construct a dialogical speech event.

ii) "Excursive": (from Latin: excurrere: to run forth or out of), the *Shorter O.E.D.* gives: 1. escape from bounds; 4. a journey from any place with the intention of returning to it; 6. deviation from a definite path or course; a digression.

This chapter undertakes a phenomonological analysis of the performance, *A Cut*, which excavates all these senses of going out (of the Gallery space), transgression (of the art-critical discourse), of a discursive process which crosses and traverses discursive boundaries and domains, of a contingent and aleatory encounter with phenomena, and of return on itself.

DISCURSIVE/EXCURSIVE *
Damian Brennan

"What is the appropriate way of dealing with signs? Taking our orientation toward the above example (the arrow), we must say that the corresponding behavior (being) toward the sign encountered is 'yielding' or 'remaining still' with reference to the approaching car which has the arrow. *As a way of taking a direction, yielding belongs essentially to the being-in-the-world of Da-sein. Da-sein is always somehow directed and under way.* Standing and remaining are only the boundary instances of this directed being 'underway'. Signs address themselves to a specifically 'spatial' being-in-the world (*emphasis added*)."[1]

"*Sinistre*. In circumstances such as these bi-pedal movement is quite simple. I place the weight of my body back onto my heels. I raise my left leg, bending the knee and transfering weight to my right hip. I project the left leg some eight or nine inches forward whilst shifting weight and my centre of balance from right to left. I am now falling forward. The heel then makes contact with the floor, followed by the arch, ball and toes.

"*Normale*. In relation to this, the weight previously legislated by the right leg is released - muscles are relaxed; the heel rises with the bending of the knee and the limb is swung forward. The right leg then initiates a mirror sequence and events become one movement. Mirror sequencing."[2]

What kind of a work is *A Cut*? In no sense is it 'site-specific'. As a process, it calls into question the applicability of the art-critical notion, site-specific. The implication of a performance understood as site-specific is that the formal meaning of the work is specifically located in a particular place. The 'artwalk'[3] of this event establishes a *rupture* within site-specfic practice.

A Cut takes place in a particular locale. The literal place however offers only *stepping off points* into a *field of discourse(s)*, out of which walkers can fashion a diversity of thematic and discursive events. These events are located in no place in particular. They are language events instantiated in the particularity of the performance. Each walk is distinct. Each performance of the walk is a different work, but each takes place within a set of discursive possibilities, traversed anew with each performance. The relation of work to site, is analogous to the relation of play-text to stage; or of music-score to performance. Each performance event opens the *field of discourse(s)* to an exploration of its discursive possibilities.

This *wound* or *insult* to the convention of the specified site or 'situated performance' is iterated thoughout the performance in its foregrounding of 'text' over place. There is a reiterated shifting of the grounds of reflection. The walkwork encompasses travel, trade, commerce, traffic, speech, language, discourse, memory, desire, death and erasure. It is a 'discursive performance' founded on the phenomenologies of walking through diverse environments, actively and dialectically unearthing and disclosing zones of being which - in their primordial and *a priori* relation to the being of the walkers/workers - *transgress*, *insult*, *rupture* normative and ideologically legitimated modes of knowing. The being of the artwalkers is implicated in the working of the walk and this is in no way a comfortable event. This being is *uncanny*, perhaps precisely because 'we' do not know who, or what 'human being' is, because, whatever it is, we *are* it. And wherever we are, we are immersed in it, and our immersion spreads across space and time.[4] Immersion in a world is not a question of location in a place. The artworkers must walk with the materials of their world: embodiment, finitude, their others, death and their inscribed and inescapable *historicality*.[5]

It is my purpose here to understand Tim Brennan's discursive performances as in no way site-specific. To the contrary, *A Cut* actively questions and rejects a naturalised assumption of the *site* as some unproblematic ground of social meaning. The *vicinity* of the Gallery is a point of entry to a network of intersubjective discourses which present a problematic for the participants. This problematic confronts them in their specific modernities. By contrast with the tales of Ovid, there is no 'genius loci' hidden in this place, to be invoked and, through art, given voice.[6] This is an entirely secularised practice. It is also a socialised and collective practice. Nor is this practice *body-centred* - 'body-centered' performance takes a body in its materiality as a *focus* of formal meaning. The body can be dead or alive.[7] It presents itself as the medium of the work, by contrast with traditional sculpture which thematises the body within a medium of representation as wood, marble, bronze. Body-centred performance engages with the body as the site of representation implicating desire and death. This practice requires a discursive context or frame.

A Cut is a walk. Bodies living, dead, anonymous and mythified, are met with *en route*. The bodies of the walkers are fundamentally implicated in the artwork/walkwork.[8] Bodies are encountered in the work. On the way, places are crossed which bodies have traversed. Various deaths are described and, in *A Cut*, a number of autopsies are introduced, together with a cremation. The body is thematised in its diverse fates as a *topos* and theme of reflection.

The performed walkwork on the occasion of Orlan's performance at Camerawork Gallery in February 1997 joined the 'audience' for this Orlan performance.[9] Orlan's body-centred performance was integrated into the walkwork horizon. Within that horizon Orlan's performance acquires a 'frame' in addition to the 'white cube' of the gallery space, and the framing Lacanian commentary integral to 'her' performance. Orlan's energetic parodying of the categories of aesthetic consumption within the classical canon takes up a position within the horizon of *A Cut*.

The multiple images or 'bodies' of Orlan join the serial bodies of the walk: the racialised, sexualised, gendered, class-stratified, cosmeticised, medicated, etc. *bodies of the walkers* in their encounter with *the bodies of the walk*: Richard Green and his Nineteenth Century project of a/his "history... of the English People" that "should never sink into a 'drum and trumpet history'"; Joseph Merrick, known as the 'Elephant Man'; Frederick Treves who 'rescued (him) from a life as a circus freak'; the reported research of Anita Sharma whose conclusion is that "his skeleton shows the tell-tale signs of Proteus Syndrome"; Ovid's telling of the metamorphic activity of Proteus, "the god who dwells in the sea that encircles the land" as one who has "the power to change into several forms"; Joseph Merrick's fairground lament, "The mis-shaped clay/The careless potter tossed aside"; Catherine Moreton, 22 year old nurse, "My father suggested I should become a nurse"; Ovid's fable of the origin of prostitution when the Propoetides women denying the divinity of Venus, thereby incurred her wrath, so "the blood hardened in their cheeks, and it required only a slight alteration to transform them into stoney flints" (Eros and Thanatos, conjunct in the stoney whiteness of flesh from which all the blood has drained); Ovid's telling of Pygmalion's sculpting 'with marvellous artistry' the perfect woman out of his disgust with prostitution; the account of Merrrick's death aged 27 "either from suffocation or dislocation of his neck due to his heavy skull falling backwards"; Ovid's account of Pygmalion's prayer to Venus and subsequent stroking of 'the object of his prayers' as he takes possession of his ideal woman; the body of Mary Anne Nicholls, Whitechapel murder victim and the details of her removal to the 'mortuary'; the views of 'male nurse' Gerry Lewis on his profession; further details of the 'examination' of Mary Ann Nicholls's cadaver; the modus operandi of the 'Ripper' in the case of Mary Ann Nicholls; a pub ornament in the style of Botticelli's *Venus*; Reg Kray's 'cultural life' including *Strangers in the Night* (which reminded him of Tangiers - 'his favourite place'); Al Luoi Chon, trainee nurse; the Cripples Band of Ragged School children; an 1848 Commissioners' Report of 'brutal cruelties' inflicted upon pauper women in the Bethnal Green Pauper Lunatic Asylum; a retelling of Trelawney's account of Williams's and then Shelley's cremations near Pisa; Sidney Frank Godley VC; the moment from Mary Shelley's *Frankenstein* when the creature comes to life; an account of the execution of the nurse Edith Cavell; the soundtrack of *My Fair Lady*, a musical adaptation of G.B. Shaw's play, *Pygmalion*, a parable about class and sexuality in London, which is a transformation of Ovid's ironic fable in the *Metamorphoses*.

The inventory of topoi, themes, quotations, textual and intertextual allusions, discursive events sketched above is attached to an *itinary*.[10] Thus in structural terms the textuality diachronically disclosed by the walk, is gathered synchronically in relations of possible signification. The jouney articulates points of connexion and disjunction both within and between discourses. The principle of textual selection is at every turn peregrinatory making space for

aleatory play of possible signification, as thrown up by the walk.
When the walks took place in February 1997 they 'ended' at
Camerawork Gallery with the exhibition of Orlan. It happened that
this body-focused performance was, in Heideggerian terms, ready-
to-hand (*zuhanden*) as a discourse to join the discourses traversed
by the walk.

PEREGRINATIONS AND PROBLEMIZATIONS

The walks in their deviation from touristic models achieve the
condition of '*peregrination*', in its primary sense of travelling in
foreign parts.[11] The familiar and local when laid bare as a matrix of
textuality, is made strange. The devices deployed to achieve this
effect, align elements of the performative practice with that
Formalist 'making strange' (*ostranenie*) which Victor Shklovsky
saw as central to poetic art: to reverse and counteract the process of
habituation and automatisation endemic in everyday modes of
perception.[12] Roman Jakobson developed a more technically
sophisticated linguistic concept of this process as the 'poetic
function' wherein, " a word is perceived as a word and not merely
as a proxy for the denoted object or an outburst of emotion, that
words and their arrangement, their meaning, their outward and
inward form, acquire weight and value of their own."[13] In the
performance, the focus on textuality, by refusing a determinate
boundary between the work and the world, by the same token,
resists any appropriation of the work on the level of the aesthetic or
purely formal. In taking its stance in the materiality of existence,
what Heidegger calls the inescapable *thrownness*[14] of Da-sein's
relationship to its world, is brought into the performance. The walk
brings us into a web of textualities which inscribe both desire and
death but does not give us any consoling narrative or authorial
pointers towards a pre-fabricated resolution, whether aesthetic or
political. The performance opens a field of discourses, ready to
hand, but without an available use. In this sense the world is both
highly discursive and, literally, without significance in itself.
Heidegger describes this 'anxiety' as "naked Da-sein as something
that has been thrown into uncanniness... it also reveals the
possibility of an authentic potentiality-for-being"[15] whereby the
future in its finitude is incorporated in Da-sein. In this there is a
similarity with Brecht's notion of an alienation effect
(*verfremdung*)[16] whereby the object of art - in this case dramaturgy-

is seen to be the revolutionary goal of making the audience aware that the institutions and social formulae which they inherit are not eternal and 'natural' but historial and man-made, and so open to transformation through human agency. The agency at hand for this redemption is the proletariat as the last opportunity of a truly human resolution inscribed and embedded in the material dialectic of history. By contrast these performances do not presuppose any direction to materiality waiting to be uncovered by the work, and as it were lying there ready to hand alongside the work.

One approach to thinking the kind of discursive play thrown up by the work is through Foucault's concept of problemization. Within a domain of action involving the body, desire and death, a process of thought might be inaugurated where our habitual and automatised preconceptions break down. As Foucault puts it, in a late interview, "for a domain of action, a behavior, to enter the field of thought, it is necessary for a certain number of factors to have made it uncertain, to have made it lose its familiarity, or to have provoked a certain number of difficulties around it. These elements result from social, economic, or political processes. But here their role is that of instigation. They can exist and perform their action for a very long time, before there is effective problemization by thought".[17]

The peregrination of the work throws up discursive possibilities which in their dispersed and scattered occurrence nevertheless group themselves into a problematic which provides no consolations but which sets up a process of thought between the walkers, their anxieties, and their inescapably historical world.

THE BODY, DESIRE AND DEATH
The inventory of bodies in the walk makes up an archive or museum of corporeality; part morgue, part waxworks, part sculpture gallery, part brothel, part cemetery - and part, with Orlan, 'tableau vivant'. The roles of 'curating' and of 'creating' are conflated and deconstructed. Tim Brennan acts as 'tour guide' or perhaps 'grammarian', but these roles are metaphoric. The role is polymorphous and shifting; and can be taken by other walkers. At times he is a kind of psychopomp (the traditional role of Hermes, patron of travellers, merchants, thieves and interpreters) leading the uninitiated into the sacred mysteries. But these strictly metaphorical

roles are the ghosts of practices not to be found here. There is no Truth at the heart of the work.

The tour introduces a diversity of discursive events and productions around these bodies in their respective socio-historical contexts, opening a zone of reflexive awareness and dialogue. The site of the work is that range of material within the ambulatory locale of the gallery. There is no aesthetic body at the centre of the walk. The horizon of the work is constituted by the Da-sein it discloses to the walkers, through their own thrownness, anxiety and finitude. The work therefore lacks any boundary that is not arbitrary and contingent. This walk/work actively rejects a naturalised assumption of the *site* as an unproblematic ground of social meaning.

The work has a contingent integrity constituted by the movement and transitory bodily instantiations of discursive acts - speech acts - and references to formations of discourse - quotations, allusions, and unspoken utterances. It draws into its textuality whole registers of discourse, and of discursive practice: demotic, gossip, oral narrative, poetic, autobiographical, philanthropic, forensic, criminological, medical historiographical, biographical, etc. The work is articulated and punctuated through acts of utterance, and the instantiation of a variety of possibilities of discourse within the horizon of the walk. The work invokes and refers to unactualised discursive formations and possibilities. The work 'lights up' this available and 'ready to hand' set of instrumentalities which are both 'in' the site and constitutive of the being-in-the world of the walkers, integral to their Da-sein.

A Cut makes multiple incisions into the 'taken for granted' everyday being of the walkers - the automatised being of the pre-understood, pre-packaged, ideologically and existentially passified being constructed by the circulation of reassuring signs within the culture. Signification unfolds within the walk/work dialectically as both a language in use and a language about use. The distinction of object and metalanguage is unstable and shifting, just as the bodies of the walkers are both inside and outside the bodies of the walk. Unlike Merrick and Shelley the walkers take leave of the walk, to be replaced by other walkers and other discursive acts. Their absence at the centre of the work simultaneously relates both the Da-sein of each walker and the being of the work to death. Roland Barthes wrote of *The Death of the Author*.[18] The logic of that position is here extended to the viewer.

The work engages with the performance of Orlan as a quoted spectacle; which takes its place as the *terminus ad quem* of the preceding discourses. The walk in this performance leads into the Orlan scene and includes it in its horizon. What can be said about the walk on the occasion of the Orlan performance? What can be said about the Orlan performance on the occasion of the walk?[19]

Over the past decade Orlan has adopted plastic surgery as a means of parodying the *atelier* system of Classical Sculpture by celebrating its 'democratisation' into the daily consumption of the female body under the signifiers of desire. So the Beauty Salon creates the Salon Art of our age. Orlan is ruthless in subverting 'ideal' spiritualities of beauty, conformity and sanctity, and relocating them in a culture of the flesh. Making her own body the material of her art, Orlan has undergone repeated 'live' cosmetic operations that have altered her facial features. The modern operating theatre thus displaces the atelier. Orlan makes reference to Botticelli's *Venus*, Gustave Moreau's *Europa*, Gerard's *Psyche*, the Fontainbleau School's *Diana* and da Vinci's *Mona Lisa*.

In the small gallery of Camerawork, in London's East End, a series of fourteen large colour 'documentary' photographs of Orlan's face in the midst of its transformation filled the white gallery space with the images of the dismantling of a face. These photographs recorded the gory procedures of her seventh operation, entitled *Omniprescence* (from the series *The Reincarnation of St.Orlan*). The spectacle of a video performance giving close-ups of the lifting of the skin of Orlan's face as a great flap of material challenged the audience to keep watching. In some ways it was an invitation to a spectacle not unlike those public scenes of torture, dismemberment and execution so characteristic of the pre-modern world. Except this was post-modern in its playing with evisceration and death. Nobody dies under the knife. Rather, as Orlan ironically displays in her tableaux vivants, she can toy with a resurrection of the flesh, that fantasy of convergence of idea and reality which fired the classical tradition, and inspired hopes of a life after death.

The sight of the semi-anaesthetised artist undergoing extensive facial reconstruction is, for most people, unbearable. The mirroring relationship which is integral to the psychology of perceiving faces is deeply insulted and traumatised by the ripping up of the face we view. The viewer is compelled to develop complex cognitive strategies of evasion to cope with the direct perception of physical trauma and facial penetration by surgical instruments. At the Lacanian level of the Imaginary, we experience our face (which we never see except as a mirror) in the ripping before us, and this disintegration, signifies the destruction of that specular and imaginary ego, which, in the Mirror Stage, as an infant had been granted to us as an omnipotent imaginary unity of the subject undivided from the body - the moment of foundation in jubilatory triumph (*jouissance*) of what will become the adult ego.[20]

The surface skin of Orlan's face is slowly peeled back from its subcutaneous fat like a large flap of red silk. As Orlan's face is unwrapped before us, we undergo compulsively this tearing away of the illusion of our oneness. The performance is an 'in-your-face' bereavement. Some fainted as the video monitor displayed the head of Orlan under the moving knife - instruments probing under her skin as the artist/patient, like some dissected ventriloquist's dummy, read Lacanian texts aloud, speaking the voice of the Analyst ("*the one who is supposed to Know*") over her own undoing.

The performance leaves the viewer without guidance as to its purpose. The audience is repeatedly confronted with Orlan's face in, and at, various stages of laceration, incision and surgical manipulation. And unlike other examples in the current aestheticisation of the dissected body, visitors are confronted with the face itself as a 'canvas', or rather, and shockingly (but ironically) with the *face of the artist* as canvas: as a placeless (and ultimately faceless) photophobic site of operation. The artwork/artist becomes a medico-aesthetic building site. The selection and layout of the various corporeal building materials: skin, subcutaneous fat, blood, offer an interpretation of the condition of woman under absolute objectification - the flesh 'insulted' and surgically transfigured; then an interpretation of absolute subjectification - the condition of woman as diva, saint, goddess or star, who chooses instrumentally the adoption of a beauty-type through the sculpting wonders of cosmetic *craft*. The trajectory of fleshly humiliation and aesthetic transcendance reaches its redeeming climax - a veritable *apotheosis* in two portraits of a red, black and blue eyed Orlan adopting the pose of St. Teresa of Avila, as portrayed in Bernini's great Baroque sculpture in in Rome (Santa Maria della Vittoria).

This erotic 'jouissance'[21] is ambivalently positioned in succession to the evisceration which is its prelude, an erasure and re-configuration of the flesh. The sequence is a profoundly dis-gusting event, which, reflexively, one knows, might signify in the code of the Beautiful, if only it could be re-appropriated within a Symbolic Register[22] which had the power to subsume and transubstantiate the fragmented body which had been displayed before us in such meticulous and intolerable detail. This particular *aufgehoben*,[23] is condemned to be defeated by the power of wounded flesh, and is only ever an empty play of a signifier at once parodistic and atheistic. The viewer is thereby caught between an insulted Imaginary and an impossible Symbolic realm. S/he is brought into a condition of being in bits, whilst seeking a wholeness, which the work simultaneously celebrates and denies. Lacan describes the 'corps morcellé' - the experience of the body in bits - as a fundamental psychotic predicament, and we are brought to this psychotic root of the subject.[24] The multiple cosmetic transformations register powerfully as a series of de-compositions.

Orlan picks up in a witticism the condition of the postmodern body: at once an object of multiple transformation and chameleon identity, and a subject without apparent history choosing as if from a supermarket the images of its next reincarnation. Underlying this consumerist mythology, is displayed a psychosis without end through which bodies are made and 'unmade' as the imaginary and the symbolic merge and diverge, in the production and destruction of the subject.[25]

This multiplication of the bodily image (imago) through mirroring (hall of mirrors) and, in this case, suffering multiple typological reconstructions of the face implicitly equates the production of art with the dominance of the metaphoric function (*jouissance*) with its dream of mergence in the Imaginary. Signification *condenses* discrete entities (the material face, the aesthetic type-face) along an axis of similarity, equivalence and fusion.[26] The type-face finds its material instantiation in Orlan's facial possibilities. Orlan like Pygmalion makes to fashion a living sculpture.[27] This antique trope is Ovidian: Orlan conducts the metamorphosis of her flesh.

Pygmalion (that 'nom du père'[28]) is a signifier seeking the presence of an absolute signified so that Truth could come and dwell with him, without that split of signifier and signified he had found in the prostitutes of the Propoetides, who, we recall, "were the first women to lose their good names by prostituting themselves in public". Here loss of name equates with loss of their place within the Symbolic Order (where identity is fused into the 'good name of the father'). Movement out of the Symbolic Order introduces a signifying field of desire gathering simultaneously and promiscuously signifier with signifier, each (metaphorically/ vertically) interchangeable with the other, and each signifier losing any transcendental (metonymic/horizontal) reference to that master Signifier Pygmalion would have for himself: 'the divinity of Venus' which they had 'denied' and which would otherwise dispose them in a chain of signification, which like a sentence bound its elements into a reference to an absent element. Pygmalion's object in making his statue is the end of desire - in a divine body, which impossibly would unite signifier with signified. In Lacanian terms, he is a jubilant infant unable to accept that the signified is only another absent signifier. Orlan acts out this madness, within the register of irony, encompassing both the fragmentation of language in the Imaginary and its psychotic identification with a transcendent signified in the order of the Symbolic. The function, in culture of the phallus as a signifier is regulative and empty. As such it founds an idea of Law, under which signifiers can be used, metaphorically, within a metonymically constituted 'signifying chain' where the body of language as a whole is absent, taking as it were the place of the absent father. As with Pygmalion or Teresa, who, in relation to that absolute 'nom du père', the divine paternal Signifier into whose emptiness Teresa pours her desire, as if, in jouissance, she had reached the end of all desire at the moment her body is enraptured in the Real Presence, Orlan acts out in this work both the driving force and the impossibility of symbolisation - the impossibility of culture itself (i.e. culture within the Imaginary Order). Outrageously she fathers herself (the impossible dream is 'autochthony'), and in her performance traces the trajectory, the cost, and the impossibilty of escaping the paternal function (which is not to be identified with biological fatherhood or patriarchy).

A Cut is a walk of about one mile beginning at The Royal London Hospital in Whitechapel and ending at Camerawork. Orlan's exhibition is now absent from the walk/work (the absence marked by a plaque in the gallery space).

METAMORPHOSIS WITHOUT A SUBJECT

The metamorphoses (metaphorical make-overs) encountered in the walk are material processes acting, as with Orlan, upon human biology; but, in these instances, unlike the practices of Orlan, the subjects undergo violent transformations without consent or choice. In that sense a perennial pre-modern predicament sets a limit to desire. Necessity (ananke) and sudden death (thanatos) figure bodies alongside desire, pleasure and *jouissance* (eros). The problemization of the body, desire and death, here finds its horizon in historicality. The focus is not intra-psychic or intra-aesthetic. The focus is discursive.

The cases encountered include Joseph Merrick who received treatment at the London Hospital; Mary Anne Nicholls, raped and murdered in 1888; Edith Cavell, shot by firing squad in 1915. The theme of the (de-)formation of bodies is explored through a number of sites. The agents of metamorphosis are several: neurofibromatosis (if Merrick's current diagnosis remains unrevised); the unknown perpetrator of the Whitechapel murders; the philanthropic foundation of 'Ragged' schools; the County Pauper Lunatic Asylum (required by parliamentary statutes) and so on.

Any walk between two points offers material on *the body*. The area of the walk has been settled since prehistoric times but underwent rapid urbanisation in the Industrial Revolution two hundred years ago. Population was heavily concentrated into a labour reserve demanded by mercantile capital for the relevant industrialisation of East London. *A Cut* is an excursion through a small segment of this East London terrain. The walk takes readings of historical residues relevant to a decoding of the body. The walkwork is structured like a montage of diverse texts and voices. It opens up rich historiographical and phenomenological layers within the event.

The result is a Bakhtinian polyphony of voices and texts.[29] The walks use found textual materials to assemble the possible conditions for the emergence of a particular *chronotope* which is Bakhtin's term for a modelling organisation of time and space, which engages with a historical and existential problematic (in the sense defined by Foucault). In this way sites can be configured as chronotopes ('chronos' meaning time, 'topos' meaning place or topic in [discourse]). Tim Brennan's 'manoeuvres' through space and time form a web of interrelated *chronotopes* (websites) amounting to what Bahktin termed *heteroglossia*. This is the manner in which the Novel gathers together diverse discourses which co-exist without being centred in a governing interpretation.[30]

The work deviates from normative expectations of genre and register. Thus the act of walking is opened to a 'trawl' of textualities, there being no reason or effort to exclude any. The walkers participate in an event constituted by discourses. Their own subject positions, voices, thoughts and viewpoints are instantiations of discursive possibilities within the field of the event. Considered as a work, it is not clear where the boundary lies, or should lie, or whether the work has or needs a boundary. These are contestable issues. The work trawls up contradictions, incompatiblities, ironies, disjunctions, and refuses resolution. The work is thereby a complex phenomenon resistant to any extorted reconciliations which privilege an authorial subjectivity over the alienating dominance of the object. It presents as what Adorno called a 'force-field' (Kraftfeld) where there is a dialectical interplay of elements but no moment of triumphant reconciliation.[31] Borrowing from Benjamin, Adorno also used the astronomical metaphor of the constellation to signify "a juxtaposed rather than integrated cluster of changing elements that resist reduction to a common denominator, essential core, or generative first principle".[32] Such an event, Tim Brennan and I describe as a *discursive performance*.

PHENOMENOLOGY AND DISCOURSE
There is an art-critical position which describes a non-gallery based

work focusing sculptural activities or forms in spaces which lack a normative aesthetic aura as site-specific work. The term is used as if it were unproblematic. It seems to convey a notion of a source of meaning which is the 'other' of art. Art when designed for a gallery context is rejected as worked out and unable to explore its own conditions of possibility, or unable to do so without repetition and an intolerable 'anxiety of influence'. By contrast site-specific work is free to tap into the non-gallery gestalts that are to be found in places, with their associated practices.

The site-specific notion that art-practice can revive itself by recourse to the meanings that are 'to hand' in places and their associated practices takes these meanings as 'given', ie. "present-at-hand".[33] This 'givenness' presupposes a centred, holistic and naturally 'whole' notion of meaning inhere-ing in places as sedimentations of lived experience and accessible to reflective consciousness. What tends to emerge is a condition in which *closure* of meaning operates as a naturalised given.

The notion of 'place' is not existentially primordial in this sense. More fundamental is Being-in-the-World, wherein 'place' gets caught up in the concerns of Da-sein. Thus in Heidegger's anlysis of Da-sein, "Regions are not first formed by things which are, present-at-hand together; they always are ready-to-hand already in individual places".[34] Human places are websites of instrumentalities, either consituting a world seamlessly connected to Da-sein or a site where Da-sein's concerns are strange to us because connected to a world which is no longer ours. Whatever is ready-to-hand for Da-sein is spatial. This is as true of the hunter gatherer, the farmer, the Fulani herdsman whose 'place' is on the move; as it is of the highly territorialised being of the man of property. Settlement is only one of Da-sein's possibilities. Heiddegerian *shelter* is an altogether less 'situated' condition, subject as it is to the ravages of climate, the failure of crops and the violence of 'man'.[35]

What matters existentially, is what kind of a world emerges from the Da-sein whose body reaches out for the equipment that lies at hand. The world of tools within which Da-sein moves and has its being, includes in the very core of its being, language in discourse.[36] There are contexts of disorientation, contexts within which individuals and groups are dissociated, places subject to defamiliarisation, historical and experiential zones that are ideologically and literally erased. Thus human places are always already hybrid. Places are made up of interlocking and conflictual histories the traces of which can be unearthed in the various worlds of equipment and discourse embedded in their materiality. Da-sein's concerns and projects can be disentangled, archaeologically, within the textual environment. There is no homogeneity within this record.

The diverse socialities of space which makes it a 'place' are just these 'traces' of 'human' intentionality, these furrows of Da-sein and its being-in-the-world.

SURFACES

Formally *A Cut* as a mode of historical research involves the idea of 'surfaces'[37] on a number of levels. One is a general corporeal focus to the walk - the skin of the body. On another level the group is conceptually moving through a congestion of discourses assembled from past and contemporary texts - the skins of languages and the bodies of texts. The act of walking traces the material surface - the built skin of a city, which marks out the pathways of bodies, some dead, some still living.

The chosen texts do not always illustrate or satisfy an expected history of each chosen location en route. At times sites or stopping points are juxtaposed with quotations in such a way as to subvert the received nature of a place. Places may then be re-configured within a horizon of critical reflection. The codes of architecture and the schemata of town planning can be foregrounded as themselves 'quotations' or 'texts' embedded in discursive practices: hospital, shop, school, asylum, morgue, alleyway, wasteland.

It is not possible or even interesting to catalogue a complete list of 'environmental texts' experienced on this walk. Such a task would involve the ability of seeing and registering everything within a given glance. It is the task of the walkers to assemble the surfaces anew each time and, within the open texture of the work, to address its problematic. Nothing is excluded, neither news, nor weather, nor traffic, nor the redevelopment of the site. The work then exists as a set of surfaces brought together by the bodies of the walkers.

67

When commenting upon developments in the late 1950's into 'textual' analysis in the West, Raymond Williams delineated an emerging gap between art and life:

"Yet what was now again being said, by nearly everyone, was that specification depended on the excision of such naiveties as 'external' content and agency, and the name for this specification was *text*. Ironically this was from the same vocabulary as the academic 'canon'. A text: an isolated object to be construed and discoursed upon: once from pulpits, now from seminar desks. Nor could it make any useful difference when this isolated object began to be opened up to its internal uncertainties and multiplicities, or to the further stage of its entire and helpless openness to any form of interpretation or analysis whatever: that cutting loose of readers and critics from any obligation to social connection or historical fact. For what was being excluded, from this work reduced to the status of text or of text as critical device, was the socially and historically specifiable agency of its making: an agency that has to include both content and intention, in relative degrees of determinancy, yet is only fully available as agency in both its internal (textual) and social and historical (in the full sense, formal) specificities."[38]

In a recent paper discussing his work, Tim Brennan has quoted this passage from Raymond Williams's "The Uses of Cultural Theory" as marking an antinomy between life and art, which subsequently has developed into a project of "articulating this division in such a way as to bring the abstract and the actual together".[39] Brennan continues that there is within historiography a "further complication": that of the division between event and memory. He cites Allessandro Portelli's essay, *The Death of Luigi Trastulli,*[40] focused on the death of an Italian steel worker. The misinformation, hearsay and myth in the construction of unfolding collective symbolic activities surrounding the man's death is itself historical, though not factual in a positivistic sense. Brennan describes his practice as a manoeuvre which resists approaches which "sever art from life, theory from practice, writing from reading, interpretation from production, mimesis from actuality and past from present from future".

My own view is that these antinomies are themselves the product of a philosophical tradition based on a subject-object dualism which is itself in need of deconstruction. My own route out of the dualism is through Heidegger and Foucault, who analyse 'human' being in terms of power and practice, temporality and discourse. Brennan's manoeuvres, on this view, enable engagements with human practices (Da-sein) in a space where the emergence of 'subjectivities' can be understood as a practical process within history.

NOTES

1. Martin Heidegger, *Being and Time, A Translation of 'Sein und Zeit'*, Translated by Joan Stambaugh (New York, 1996), p.74. This passage from Section 17, 'Reference and Signs' provides a phenomenological analysis of the being of signification as a constitutive function of Da-sein's being-in-the-world. The original work was published in 1927. This translation is of the 1953 (Tubingen) edition. It builds on the translation by John Macquarrie & Edward Robinson (Oxford 1962), where this passage can be found on p.110.

2. From Tim Brennan's Journal for June 1990

3. 'Art-walk': throughout, I refer to the performance, as variously art-work, art-walk, work-walk. As the practice of the performance works out of the being-in-the-world of the participants - their Da-sein, the performance might best be characterised as an 'art-work/walk-work'. This understands the constitutive elements of the practice as, together, making up a mode of being. This would be, in Heideggerian terms, a founded mode, in which the elements can subsist only when connected with something else, in this case, a world of (discursive) practices sketched out in the compound phrase. See Macquarrie & Robinson, p.86 note 1.

4. See, *Being and Time*, Stambaugh, op.cit. p.342, 'However, death is, after all, only the "end" of Da-sein, and formally speaking, it is just *one* of the ends that embraces the totality of Da-sein. But the other 'end' is the "beginning", "birth". Only the being "between" birth and death presents the whole we are looking for'. The predicament of 'being between', or as in the generic opening for Epic 'in medias res', 'in the middest', conditions those 'lines of desire' and longing which drive both migration and history. For a remarkable meditation on time and fiction, see Frank Kermode, *Sense of an Ending: studies in the theory of fiction* (Ann Arbor, 1967). For 'lines of desire" see Tim Brennan "Manoeuvre, Discursive Performance" (presently in manuscript) p2:

"...town planners have often used the term 'lines of desire' to describe those paths or tracks produced by people taking repeated short*cuts* across land".

5. I have retained the Macquarrie & Robinson translation of Heidegger's 'geschichtlichkeit' in preference to Stambaugh's 'historicity' to emphasise the inescapable and primordial character of this feature of 'human' being in time,and to keep it fully free from any notion of its depending on a discipline of history, or any specific connection to 'pastness' as such. Historicality includes the past, the present and the future. It is that intersection of the self-construed fate (Schicksal) of an individual with the predicament or 'destiny' (Geschick) of their construed community. Historicality would interrogate the individual as to its engagement within the struggles which motivate social and political action. See, Stambaugh, op.cit. p.344: "The specific *movement of* the *stretched out stretching itself along*, we call the *occurrence* of Da-sein. The question of the "connectedness" of Da-sein is the ontological problem of its occurrence. To expose the "*structure of the occurrence*" and the existential and temporal conditions of its possibility means to gain an *ontological* understanding of historicity" (viz 'historicality').

6. The topos of the Genius Loci, as it comes down to us from Graeco-Latin literature, and its relation to the contemplation of death in wayside inscriptions on memorial stelae is brilliantly explored by Geoffrey Hartmann in his "Inscriptions and Romantic Nature Poetry", in *Beyond Formalism* (New Haven, 1970). This particular tradition which is active in Romantic nature and loco-descriptive poetry connects the Epitaph in the landscape (a literal inscription) with the tutelary guardianship of the genius loci, or patron god/spirit of that place (say, a Grove or Spring). In Wordsworth, the tutelary spirit is translated into the presiding genius of the Creative Imagination as incarnated in both the 'author's' synthetic powers and the immanent spirit of Nature. The author 'dies into' this impersonal and sublime power within himself. In Discursive Performance the Romantic author or Creative Artist is dead. This is an entirely secularised practice. It is also a socialised and collective practice.

7. For example, the case of Anthony-Noel Kelly recently put on trial for stealing body parts and cadavers from the Royal College of Surgeons, in order to make out of them plaster casts. See Brian Masters in *The Observer*, 29 March 1998, p.5. I need not mention, in this context, the oeuvre of Damien Hirst which stops short of the genre of body-snatching rediscovered in the intriguing forensic history of Mr Kelly.

8. See note 3 above.

9. The title of Orlan's exhibition is: *Orlan: This Is My Body, This Is My Software* Camerawork, January 17 - 22 February 22, 1997

10. For the texts presented in the walk see: *A Cut* herein.

11. "Peregrination"; see: *The Shorter O.E.D.* which gives the sense as, "The action of travelling in foreign parts... from place to place". Also " ... peregrinations about this great metropolis 1820".

12. For Victor Shlovsky's 'ostranenie', often translated as 'defamiliarisation', but perhaps more accurately, 'making strange', see his 'Art as Technique' in Lemon, Lee & Reis, Marion J. (ed. & trans.), *Russian Formalist Criticism: Four Essays* (Lincoln: University of Nebraska Press, 1965); and Matejka, Ladislav and Pomorska, Krystyna (eds), *Readings in Russian Poetics: Formalist and Structuralist Views* (Cambridge, Mass.: M.I.T. Press, 1971); Todorov, Tzvetan (ed.), *Théorie de la litterature: textes des formalistes russes* (Paris: Seuil 1965). For an overview of Russian Formalism, see Erlich,Victor, *Russian Formalism: History-Doctrine* (The Hague, 1955 rev. ed. 1965).

13. For Roman Jakobson's 'poetic function', see his 'Closing Statement: Linguistics and Poetics', of the Indiana Conference on Style, reprinted in Sebeok, Thomas A. ed., *Style in Language* (Cambridge, Mass. 1960), pp.350-377. This is a standard point of reference for recent work in

the field. Jakobson is also represented in the above anthologies, see note 10.

14. "Thrownness", a translation of Martin Heidegger's 'Geworfenheit'. For the "inescapable thrownness of Da-sein", cf: Macquarrie & Robinson, trans. *Sein und Zeit*, p.321, "Yet every Da-sein always exists factically, it is not a free-floating self-projection; but its character is determined by thrownness as a Fact of the entity which it is; and, as so determined, it has in each case already been delivered over to existence, and it constantly so remains. Da-sein's facticity, however, is essentially distinct from something present-at-hand within the world. But neither does thrownness adhere to Da-sein as an inaccessible characteristic which is of no importance for its existence. As something thrown, Da-sein has been thrown into existence. It exists as an entity which has to be as it is and as it can be."

15. Macquarrie & Robinson, trans., *Sein und Zeit*, p.394. The uncanny in this translation corresponds to the German, 'unheimlich'. See p.233, "In anxiety one feels *'uncanny'*. Here the peculiar indefiniteness of that which Da-sein finds itself alongside in anxiety, comes proximally to expression: the 'nothing and nowhere'. But here 'uncanniness' also means 'not-being-at-home'". Anxiety resides in that feeling of unfamiliarity in a place we assumed we knew well, but which has undergone loss of this character of a world in which we are absorbed, unreflexively, through our everyday concerns. We are now in an un-homely place. Thus Shlovsky's function of art: 'ostranenie', is an existential component of our being-in-the-world. In the literal sense of peregrination as travelling abroad in a strange place, the walk-work brings us to an uncanny experience of estrangement from a world we took for granted. This is also a signifier of death, and, by the same token, of a possibility for authentic being.

16. For Bertoldt Brecht and 'verfremdung', see Walter Benjamin, *Understanding Brecht*, trans. Anna Bostock (London, New Left Books 1973).

17. Michel Foucault, "Polemics, Politics, and Problemization", in Paul Rabinow, ed., *The Foucault Reader* (Harmondsworth, Penguin Press, 1983), p.388. For Foucault's late notion of 'problemization', see Thomas Flynn, "Foucault's Mapping of History", p.37, in Gary Gutting, (ed.), *The Cambridge Companion to Foucault* (Cambridge, 1994). Michael Schwartz has drawn my attention to the importance of Heidegger in the formation of Foucault's thought, "As the crux of Foucault's final redescription (of his entire life work as concerned with problemization), the notion of problemization can be grasped as a creative reworking of Heidegger's account of equipmental deficiency", which was Heidegger's description of our coming to thought at the point where the practical constitution of our modes of being breaks down, and we can no longer utilise what is 'ready to hand' unreflectively. See Michael Schwartz, "Critical Reproblemization: Foucault and the Task of Modern Philosophy", in *Radical Philosophy*, 91, Sept/Oct 1998, pp.19-29.

18. Roland Barthes, "The Death of the Author" in *Image, Music, Text*, translated by Stephen Heath (London, Fontana 1977) pp.142-148. See p.142, "writing is the destruction of every voice, of every point of origin." Also, p.145, "Linguistically, the author is never more than the instance saying I : language knows a 'subject', not a 'person', and this subject, empty outside of the very enunciation which defines it, suffices to make language 'hold together', suffices, that is to say, to exhaust it". And, again, p.147, "*writing* .... by refusing to assign a 'secret', an ultimate meaning, to the text (and to the world as text) liberates what may be called an anti-theological activity, an activity that is truly revolutionary since to refuse to fix a meaning is, in the end, to refuse God and his hypostases - reason, science, law." And on the reader, see p.148: "he is simply that *someone* who holds together in a single field all the traces by which the written text is constituted". Barthes' characterisation of *a text* as "made up of multiple writings, drawn from many cultures and entering into mutual relations of dialogue, parody, and contestation" accords exactly with the multivocality of discursive performance in *A Cut*, and the role of the participant performer is also indicated in Barthes' description of the Reader as the "one *place* where this multiplicity is focused...The reader is the space on which all the quotations that make up the writing are inscribed without any of them being lost; a text's unity lies not in its origin but in its destination". See p.148. One argument of this chapter proposes that the *place* or *site* of the performance is its *intertextuality* in Barthes' sense. See footnotes 30-32 below.

19. Orlan, see Duncan McCorquodale (ed.), *Ceci est mon corps... Ceci est mon logiciel... (This is My Body...This Is My Software...)*, Black Dog, 1996, pp.88-89.

20. For the Mirror Stage, see Jacques Lacan, "Le stade du mirroir comme formateur de la fonction du Je", *Revue francaise de psychanalyse* (1949) 4, pp.449-455. Also in Alan Sheridan (trans.), *Écrits: A Selection* (London, Tavistock Publications Ltd. 1977), pp.1-7 as "The mirror stage as formative of the function of the I". See p.2, "This jubilant assumption of his specular image by the child at the *infans* stage, still sunk in his motor incapacity and nurseling dependence, would seem to exhibit in an exemplary fashion the symbolic matrix in which the I is precipitated in a primordial form, before it is objectified in the dialectic of identification with the other, and before language restores to it, in the universal, its function as subject." Malcolm Bowie comments perceptively, "The mirror stage (*stade du mirroir*) is not a mere epoch in the history of the individual but a stadium (*stade*) in which the battle of the human subject is permanently being waged". Orlan by a repetition (compulsion) reinstates the splitting of the subject (of the viewer), a viewer whose internal division is masked in the specularity of the ego - as an illusory unity of signifier and signified. See Malcolm Bowie, *Lacan* (London, Fontana 1991) p.21.

21. See, *Écrits: A Selection*, trans., Sheridan, "Translator's note", p.x: "JOUISSANCE (*jouissance*). There is no adequate translation in English of this word. 'Enjoyment' conveys the sense, contained in *jouissance*, of enjoyment of rights, of property etc. Unfortunately, in modern English, the word has lost the sexual connotations it still retains in French. (*Jouir* is slang for 'to come'.) 'Pleasure', on the other hand, is pre-empted by '*plaisir*' - and Lacan uses the two words quite differently. 'Pleasure' obeys the law of homeostasis that Freud evokes in "Beyond the Pleasure Principle", whereby, through discharge, the psyche seeks the lowest possible level of tension. '*Jouissance*' transgresses this law and, in that respect, it is *beyond the pleasure principle*".

22. Lacan works with three interdependent terms: the Imaginary, Symbolic and the Real (*imaginaire, symbolique, réel*). See Sheridan, ibid. p.ix: "... Lacan regarded the 'imago' as the proper study of psychology and identification as the fundamental psychical process. The imaginary was then the world, the register, the dimension of images, conscious or unconscious, perceived or imagined. In this respect, 'imaginary' is not simply the opposite of 'real'.... The notion of the 'symbolic'... (does not refer to) icons, stylized figurations, but signifiers, in the sense developed by Saussure and Jakobson, extended into a generalized definition: differential elements, in themselves without meaning, which acquire value only in their mutual relations, and forming a closed order...it is the symbolic, not the imaginary, that is seen to be the determining order of the subject...In particular the relation between the subject, on the one hand, and the signifiers, speech, language, on the other, is frequently contrasted with the imaginary relation, that between the ego and its images..." Access to the Symbolic register for the infant comes via the 'paternal function' 'in the name of the father', see note 27 below.

23. See Jacques Lacan, "... the Hegelian utterances, even if one confines oneself to the text of them, are propitious for saying always an Other-thing. An Other-thing that corrects their linkage by phantasmic synthesis, while at the same time preserving the effect they have of exposing identifications in their illusoriness...this is our personal *Aufhebung*, which transforms that of Hegel, which was his personal illusion, into an opportunity to pick out, instead and in place of the leaps of an ideal progress, the avatars of a lack". Quoted and translated by Bowie (op.cit. p.97). Orlan's ostensible text is an Hegelian progress/reincarnation. This is undercut at every point with an atheistic ironic meta-text.

24. For 'corps morcellé' or 'fragmented body', as a moment in the dialectical drama of the Mirror Stage, see J. Lacan, in Sheridan, op.cit. p.4.: " I am led, therefore, to regard the function of the mirror-stage as a particular case of the function of the *imago*, which is to establish a relation betwen the organism and its reality - or, as they say, between the *Innenwelt* and the *Umwelt*... This development is experienced as a temporal dialectic that decisively projects the formation of

the individual into history. The *mirror stage* is a drama whose internal thrust is precipitated from insufficiency to anticipation - and which manufactures for the subject, caught up in the lure of spatial identification, the succession of phantasies that extends from a fragmented body-image to a form of its totality that I call orthopaedic - and, lastly, to the assumption of the armour of an alienating identity, which will mark with its rigid structure the subject's entire mental development..." Orlan's performances literalise the orthopaedic metaphor in physically aligning her body with aesthetic models to undo her deformity (cf: Procrustes). Her performance ranges across the dialectical span of 'corps morcellé' and orthopaedic repair. As such it is a living critique and an ironic celebration of 'armoured identity'. The audience suffers a knowledge it resists and has repressed. Bowie (op.cit. p.26) puts this well " The body once seemed dismembered, all over the place, and the anxiety associated with this memory fuels the individual's desire to be the possessor and resident of a secure bodily 'I'." See also Lacan's virtuoso treatement of the theme in his, 'Aggressivity in psychoanalysis' in (Sheridan, pp.8-29). As Bowie comments (op.cit. p.28), "Caught between delusional wholeness and infernal disintegration, the ego leads a doomed life". Bowie (op.cit. p.28) also notes the problem with this - which I take to be a result of Lacan's Symbolic Order being conceptualised, after Saussure, as a closed and complete system without historicality: "Whatever it is that gives the ego its normal bouyancy, and allows the individual to do such things as formulate and execute a plan, has been moved to the margins of the theoretical picture".

25. Malcolm Bowie is admirably lucid in his explication of the relationship of the Mirror-stage to the production of culture. op.cit, p.24-25, "The mirror-bemused infant , setting forth on his career of delusional ego-building, is condemned to the madness of the madhouse (*aliénation*): Lacan does not spare the child these rigours. But the *Entfremdung* of Hegel and Marx, familiarly translated into French as aliénation, provides the infant's wretchedness with a certain philosophical dignity...Lacan's usage contrasts sharply with, say, Marx's in the *Economic and Philosophical Manuscripts* or in the *Grundrisse*. For Marx the alienation of the individual from his labour, not only acts as a prototype for all other alienated relationships (between man and nature, between the individual and society, between the individual and his own body) but gives a clear indication of where the route towards reintegration lies. The migration of the term from level to level helps him to produce both an extremely broad map of human society and a cogent political message. *For Lacan, on the other hand, the prototypical alienation that occurs at the mirror stage is seen weaving its way through society* (my emphasis)." The thrust of my argument in this chapter is that *A Cut* is an instance of a kind of performative practice which, through its engagement with discourse and historicality, lays bare the problematic, without offering a diagnosis or a necessary political direction. Bowie continues his exposition: "He starves his hypothesis of the clinical data that could test its organizing power, and produces neither map nor message".

26. Here I follow Lacan's use of the two rhetorical devices: metaphor and metonymy, to redescribe Freud's "Traumdeutung" - the dream-work of *The Interpretation of Dreams* (1900, Penguin ed. 1976) p.381. f. See Jacques Lacan, "The agency of the letter in the unconscious or reason since Freud", in Sheridan, op.cit, p.160: "But what we call the two 'sides' of the effect of the signifier on the signified are also found here. *Verdichtung*, or 'condensation', is the structure of the superimposition of the signifiers, which metaphor takes as its field, and whose name, condensing in itself the word *Dichtung*, shows how the mechanism is conatural with poetry to the point that it envelops the traditional function proper to poetry. In the case of *Verschiebung*, 'displacement', the German term is closer to the idea of veering off of signification that we see in metonymy, and which from its first appearance in Freud is represented as the most appropriate means used by the unconscious to foil censorship." As Bowie (op.cit. p.71-72) comments: "There is, for analytic purposes, no bio-energetic power-house 'behind' or 'beneath' human speech, and there is no veiled signified-in-waiting that will eventually call the crazy procession of signifiers to order". Lacan's redescription of Freud's dream-work is based on Roman Jakobson and Morris Halle's seminal paper, "Two Aspects of Language and Two Types of Aphasic Disorder" in their *Fundamentals of Language* (The Hague, Mouton & Co. 1956) pp.69-96. For detailed commentaries on Lacan's use of linguistic and rhetorical theory, see Anthony Wilden, *The Language of the Self* (Baltimore, Johns Hopkins Press, 1968) which is a translation and

commentary on the Lacan paper above. Also useful is Anika Lemaire, *Jacques Lacan* (1970) trans. David Macey (London, Routledge & Kegan Paul, 1977) pp.191-205. To put it very simply: in Lacan's appropriation of Jakobsonian structural linguistics, the signifier is disposed either according to an axis of substitution and superimposition (metaphor/condensation) or combination and contiguity (metonymy/displacement).

27. I am referring here to Ovid, *Metamorphoses* Book X (1955, London,Penguin, trans. Mary, M. Innes pp.231-232) as incorporated in *A Cut*. See Chapter 2, pp.21 & 23 above, which gives the passage. The construction of another (ideal) body as in Pygmalion and Orlan is best understood as a response to the fragmented body, the point at which the mirror stage should come to an end with the identification with the 'counterpart', but when a narcissistic effort is made to reconstitute the original specular ego by freezing, foreshortening and incorporating/ingesting the counterpart: "This moment in which the mirror-stage comes to an end inaugurates, by the identification with the *imago* of the counterpart and the drama of primordial jealousy... the dialectic that will henceforth link the I to socially elaborated situations" (Sheridan, p.5). See also Bowie (ibid. p.26): "the child, itself so recently born, gives birth to a monster: a statue, an automaton, a fabricated thing...in terms that Dr. Frankenstein would have found familiar. From spare parts , an armoured mechanical creature is being produced within the human subject, and developing unwholesome habits and destructive appetites of its own. The self-division of the subject, first revealed to Freud in dreams, is here being re-imagined by Lacan as nightmare".

28. The 'name of the father' or 'nom du père' is "the symbol of an authority at once legislative and punitive. It represented, within the Symbolic, that which made the Symbolic possible - all those agencies that placed restrictions on the infant's desire and threatened to punish, by castration, infringements of their law. It was the inaugurating agent of Law, but also gave birth to the mobility and supple interconnectedness of the signifying chain" (Bowie, op.cit. p.108). Pygmalion identifies his own body as the phallus, thereby foreclosing the phallus of the absent father (nom du père): an intersubjective function that could symbolise his imaginary ego in another register. Foreclosing the Name-of-the-Father, on this account, is foundational for psychosis. See Jacques Lacan, "On a question preliminary to any possible treatment of psychosis", (Sheridan, op.cit. p.217): "For the psychosis to be triggered off, the Name-of-the-Father, *verworfen*, foreclosed, that is to say, never having attained the place of the Other, must be called into symbolic opposition to the subject... It is the lack of the Name-of-the Father in that place which, by the hole that it opens up in the signified, sets off the cascade of reshapings of the signifier (*the artificer's creative fury*: my addition) from which the increasing danger of the imaginary proceeds, until the level is reached at which signifier and signified are stabilized in the delusional metaphor", - his crazy statuary creation, an entirely imaginary grandiose extension of his penis. Pygmalion, under this account, harbours murderous impulses towards women in his lack of access to the 'nom du père' and in this sense is aligned with the Whitechapel murderer who visits his fragmentation upon his victims in order to concretise himself as the incarnation of the Law: the avenger of the fragmented male child suffering an unresolved memory of castration terror. By contrast Shaw writes a Pygmalion comedy. Eliza Doolittle (sic) is a street-walking Covent Garden flower girl (thus he transforms, metaphorically Ovid's whores). Professor Higgins changes her identity by becoming her 'analyst', and representing for her an absent father, who teaches her to speak ("properly": this is an orthopaedic task). Thus psychotic tragedy (a la Whitechapel) is transformed via the proprieties of Class into a 'comedy of manners', and Eliza becomes all that a lady should be. Orlan sets up a gigantic joke whereby she assumes the enfleshment of the Law only in order to parodise herself through the analytic discourse she intones. She does so from a place beyond Tragedy and Comedy, a place where the undone subject can be understood without psychosis. The name of her father is Lacan (but only as signifier). As Bowie says (ibid. p.109), "The Name-of-the-Father is the 'paternal metaphor' that inheres in symbolization and thereby potentiates the metaphorical process as a whole; and it is an essential point of anchorage for the subject".

29. The reference is to Mikhail Bakhtin's work on the novel. Bakhtin contrasted homophonic (monologic) texts which presuppose an old universe of "finitude and closure" characterised by

ideological centralisation and a new universe which was relativistic and open. "The problems encountered by the author and his consciousness in the polyphonic novel are far deeper, and more complex than those found in the homophonic (monologic) novel. Einstein's world possesses a far deeper and more complex unity than Newton's, of a qualitatively different order". And again, "When cultures and tongues had interanimated each other, language became altogether different; its very quality altered: instead of a Ptolomaic linguistic world, unified, singular, and closed, there appeared a Galilean universe made of a multiplicity of tongues, mutually animating each other". Quoted on pp.14-15, of Tzvetan Todorov, *Mikhail Bakhtin: the Dialogical Principle* (Manchester University Press, 1984) translated by Wlad Godzich from Todorov, *Michaïl Bahktine: le principe dialogique suivi de Écrits du Cercle de Bahktine* (Paris, Editions du Seuil, 1981).

30. Bahktin developed his concept of *chronotope* out of his notion of genre understood as a 'field of respesentation'. As he says "genre and generic species are precisely determined by the chronotope" which is the particular organisation of time and space which constitutes a given world (see Todorov, op.cit. p.83). Tim Brennan, in his paper, "Manoeuvre - Discursive Performance" (p.7) has appropriated this concept to the walk-work, which shares with Bahktin's conception of the Novel genre, an interest in *heteroglossia* - the coexistence within one field of diverse languages and discourses, unsubsumed by a master discourse (see op.cit. p.56). See also Mikhail Bahktin, *Formy vremi i khronotopa v romane*, (1937-38) trans. by Caryl Emerson & Michael Holquist, as: *Dialogic Imagination* (Austin, University of Texas, 1981), pp.84-258.

31. See Theodor W, Adorno, *Aesthetic Theory*, Ed, Gretel Adorno & Rolf Tiedemann, ed. & trans. Robert Hullot-Kentor, (Minneapolis, 1997), pp.143. f. "... aesthetic form is the objective organisation within each artwork of what appears as bindingly eloquent. It is the non-violent synthesis of the diffuse that nevertheless preserves it as what it is in its divergences and contradictions, and for this reason form is actually an unfolding of truth. A posited unity, it constantly suspends itself as such: essential to it is that it interrupts itself through its other just as the essence of its coherence is that it does not cohere. In its relation to its other-whose foreigness it mollifies and yet maintains - form is what is anti-barbaric in art; through form art participates in the civilisation that it criticises by its very existence. Form is the law of the transfiguration of the existing, counter to which it represents freedom". See also Martin Jay, *Adorno*, (Fontana , 1984) p.14.

32. Also see Martin Jay, ibid. p.15.

33. In Heiddeger's understanding the object of a natural science is to describe and measure what is 'present-to-hand' (vorhanden). But this is not what is given to Da-sein. Rather Da-sein relates to a world of equipment which is always ready-to-hand (zuhanden). Only at the point of break-down - when the hammer is broken - is it brought before Da-sein in the mode of presence-to-hand. See, for example his discussion of 'remoteness" (Macquarrie & Robinson, pp.140-1): "...the pathways we take towards desevered entities in the course of our dealings will vary in their length from day to day. What is ready-to-hand within the environment is certainly not present-at-hand for an eternal observer exempt from Da-sein... A pathway which is long 'Objectively' can be much shorter than one which is 'Objectively' shorter still but which is perhaps 'hard going' and comes before us as interminably long. *Yet only in this coming before us is the current world authentically ready- to-hand*. The Objective distances of Things present-at-hand do not coincide with the remoteness and closeness of what is ready-to-hand within-the-world..." The equipmental mode of the ready-to-hand is primordial to being-in-the-world. Meanings are not 'given' in an objectified mode.

34. See Macquarrie & Robinson, p.137, 'region' is their transaltion of Heidegger's 'Gegend'. Thus regionality is a function of equipmental complexes which are ready-to-hand (zu-handen) to Da-sein within its world. They are not aggregations of present-to-hand (vor-handen) things.

35. See, for example, Heidegger's "Building Dwelling Thinking" in *Vortrage und Aufsatze*, (Pfulling: Gunther Neske Verlag, 1954), trans. by Albert Hofstadter as *Poetry, Language,*

Thought, (New York, Harper and Row, 1971), pp.145-62: "The truck driver is at home on the highway, but he does not have his lodgings there; the working woman is at home in the spinning mill, but does not have her dwelling there; the chief engineer is at home in the power station, but he does not dwell there... Thus dwelling would in any case be the end that presides over all building. Dwelling and building are related as end and means."

36. For the primordiality of discourse in Heidegger, & Macquarrie and Robinson, op.cit. pp.203-210. As Heidegger says (p.203): "Discourse is existentially equiprimordial with state-of-mind and understanding", by which he means that these three conditions co-exist to make possible any conceivable world for Da-sein. Again, (p.204), "Language is a totality of words - a totality in which discourse has a 'worldly' Being of its own; and as an entity within-the-world, this totality thus becomes something which we may come across as ready-to-hand". The ready-to-hand, or equipmental structures of discourse are mapped by Foucault as discursive formations in such works as *The Order of Things*, trans. Alan Sheridan (London, Tavistock, 1970) *The Origins of the Clinic*, trans. Alan Sheridan (London, Tavistock, 1973).

37. Walter Benjamin famously proposed writing a book consisting solely of quotations to undermine the privilege of the authorial subject and demonstrate the collective textuality which informs writing.

38. Raymond Williams, *The Politics of Modernism*, (London, Verso, 1989), p.172.

39. Tim Brennan, "Manoeuvre - Discursive Performance", in *Writing & Making*, (conference, University of Plymouth, September 1998).

40. Alesandro Portelli, *The Death of Luigi Trastulli and Other Stories: Form and Meaning in Oral History* (SUNY Series in Oral and Public History, Albany, State University of New York, 1991), pp.1-26.

#3
A
WEAVE

1 Spitalfields, a district and parish in the east of London, between Bishopsgate and Bethnal Green, inhabited by weavers of silk and other poor people. It was a place of sepulture for Roman London, and received its name from the fields having once belonged to the Priory and Hospital of St. Mary Spital, founded in 1197 by Walter Brune and Rosia his wife, and dedicated to the honour of Jesus Christ and the Virgin Mary by the name of Domus Dei et Beate Mariae, extra Bishopsgate, in the parish of St. Botolph. Hence the present parish of Christ Church, Spitalfields. The old name was Lolesworth, according to Stow, who gives a long and particular account of the discovery of a large number of Roman cinerary urns, bones, vestiges of coffins and various other remains made in excavating on the east side of the church for brick-earth in 1576. Stow was himself present during some of the diggings, and carried with him a small 'pot of white earth... made in the shape of a hare squatted upon her legs, and between her ears the mouth of the pot; also the lower jaw of a man, some iron nails,' etc. The fields were covered with buildings between 1650 and 1660.

2 That other
That, in pure madrigal, unto his mother
Commended the French hood and scarlet gown
The Lady May'ress passed in through the town,
Unto the Spittle Sermon.

1. Henry Benjamin Wheatley *London Past & Present: Its History, Associations, and Traditions*, J. Murray, 1891, p.291

2. Ben Jonson *Underwoods (Consisting of Divers Poems)*, No.1, University Press: Cambridge, 1905, lxi.

Straight ahead. Stop at No. 19 (the home of Raphael Samuel 1934-1996). Straight ahead. Turn right onto Fleur de Lis St. Text 3. Straight ahead. Cross Commercial St. Bare right then left onto Calvin St. Straight ahead. Pause at the junction to Grey Eagle St. Look right. Text 4. Turn left onto Grey Eagle St.

3 The silk-weavers of London, and especially of Spitalfields, have lived in periodic distress for a long time, and that they still have no cause to be satisfied with their lot is proved by their taking a most active part in English labour movements in general, and in London ones in particular. The distress prevailing among them gave rise to the fever which broke out in East London, and called forth the Commission for Investigating the Sanitary Condition of the Labouring Class. But the last report of the London Fever Hospital shows that this disease is still raging.

'In 1870, when the promulgation of the celebrated decree of papal infallibility been resolved upon, it was deemed necessary that the Pope should wear at the ſdant ceremony a new vestment woven entirely in one piece. Italy, France, other European countries were vainly searched for a weaver capable of executing work, and at last the order came to England, where in Spitalfields was found only man able to make the garment, and he, by a strange irony of fate, one of erstwhile persecuted Huguenot race."—Booth's *Labour and Life of the People*, 9, vol. i. p. 394, *note*.

4 The Dollonds were French refugees, and John Dollond, the inventor of the achromatic telescope, was born in Spitalfields and worked with his father at the loom. In the churchyard of the priory (now Spital Square), was a pulpit cross, 'somewhat like,' says Stow, 'to that in St. Pauls churchyard,' where the celebrated Spital sermons were originally preached. The cross was rebuilt in 1594, and destroyed during the troubles of Charles I.

The sermons, however, have been continued to the present time, and are still preached every Easter Monday and Easter Tuesday, before the Lord Mayor and Aldermen, at Christ Church, Newgate Street. The Christ's Hospital or Blue Coat Boys were regular attendants, in the reign of Queen Elizabeth, at Spital sermons at the old cross in Spital Square.

3. Friedrich Engels *The Condition of The Working Class in England*, first published 1845, republished, Penguin Classics, 1987, p.210.
4. *The Collins English Dictionary*, William Collins Sons & Co., 1990.

5 One set of manufacturers secured to themselves special seigniorial rights over the children of the proletariat, just as they had done before. These were the silk manufacturers. In 1833 they had howled threateningly that 'if the liberty of the working children of any age for 10 hours a day were taken away, it would stop their works' (Reports of the Inspectors of Factories... 30 September 1844, p.13.). It would be impossible for them to buy a sufficient number of children over 13. They extorted the privilege they desired. Subsequent investigation showed that the pretext was a deliberate lie. This did not, however, prevent them, throughout the following decade, from spinning silk for 10 hours a day out of the blood of little children who had to be put on stools to perform their work (Report of the Inspectors of Factories... 30 September 1844, p.13.). The Act of 1844 certainly 'robbed' the silk manufacturers of the 'liberty' of employing children under 11 for longer than 6 1/2 hours each day. But as against this, it secured them the privilege of working children between 11 and 13 for 10 hours a day, and annulling in their case the education which had been made compulsory for all factory children. This time the pretext was 'the delicate texture of the fabric in which they were employed, requiring a lightness of touch, only to be acquired by their early introduction to these factories' (Reports of the Inspectors of Factories... 31 October 1846, p.20). The children were quite simply slaughtered for the sake of their delicate fingers, just as horned cattle are slaughtered in southern Russia for their hides and their fat.

eidegenoss a confederate

5. Karl Marx, *Das Kapital* , Vol 1, first published 1867, republished Penguin, 1976, p.406.

6 White Mulberry. 'Morus alba' is a deciduous tree, native to China but cultivated for centuries in other eastern countries and southern Europe for silk manufacture. Its height reaches about 9 metres. The male and female flowers, in separate catkins, are produced in May. The fruits are generally white or pink, but occasionally purple, and the shiny leaves are less downy than the Common Mulberry.

7 emporium. a large and often ostentatious retail shop offering for sale a wide variety of merchandise. [C16: from Latin, from Greek emporion, from emporos merchant, from poros a journey]

1870, when the promulgation of the celebrated decree of papal infallibility resolved upon, it was deemed necessary that the Pope should wear at the ceremony a new vestment woven entirely in one piece. Italy, France, European countries were vainly searched for a weaver capable of executing , and at last the order came to England, where in Spitalfields was found man able to make the garment, and he, by a strange irony of fate, one of while persecuted Huguenot race."—Booth's *Labour and Life of the People*, l. i. p. 394, *note*.

A Saxon Gift

One of the earliest records of silk mentioned in the Saxon chronicles is that of:

Offa, King of Mercia, received a present of two silken vests from the Emperor Charlemagne in 790.

King Alfred is also said to have had amongst his royal treasures a few garments embroidered with silk, or woven of that material.

6. Roger Phillips, *The Photographic Guide to Identify Native and Common Trees*, Elm Tree Books/Hamish Hamilton Ltd., 1986, p.99.
7. Wheatley, op.cit. p.292.

Right onto Cheshire St. Text 8. Straight ahead. Third left onto Hereford St. Right at end. Cross Buckfast St. Right onto Voss St. Straight ahead. Cross Vallance Rd. Straight ahead. Cross Hague St. Straight ahead. Cross Derbyshire St. Straight ahead. Cross Viaduct St. Left onto Seabright St. Right onto Bethnal Green Rd.

8 The silk manufacture was planted in Spitalfields by French emigrants, expelled from their own country upon the revocation of the Edict of Nantes in 1685, a measure which transferred to this country the families of Auriol, Barre, Boileau, Bouverie, Ligonier, Labouchere, Romilly, Houblon, Lefroy, Levesque, De la Haye, Garnault, Ouvry, etc. In Spitalfields are found many French names, as Bataille, Lafontaine, Strachan, Fonteneau, etc., by wavers, enamellers, jewellers, etc., both masters and workpeople, down to our own day; while still more, perhaps, translations of the original French names of their ancestors, as Masters (Le Maitre), Young (Le Jeune), Black (Lenoir), King (Le Roi), and the like; but the traces of French descent have been fast fading away in recent years.

Twisted

The cocoons are unravelled and the filaments from several twisted together; processing this raw silk includes combining these strands, washing away the sticky sericin secretion, and sometimes adding metallic salts for weight. Silk production was first practised in China.

A wide green was formed S. of the Old Ford Rd., the old NE. exit from L.; and about this green the hamlet rose. Bishop's Hall, a one-time residence of the Bps. of L., stood in the NE. on ground now part of Victoria Park, and the remaining portion was pulled down on the formation of the park, opened in 1844. Another notable mansion was Bethnall House or Kirby's Castle, built by John Kirby, a L. citizen, in the time of Elizabeth. It was known as 'the Blind Beggar's House.' In Pepys' time it belonged to Sir Wm. Ryder, Deputy Master of Trinity House, and in it Pepys deposited most of his valuables at the time of the G.F.

8. Wheatley, op.cit. pp.291-292

Cross Bethnal Green Rd. Straight ahead. Left onto Punderson Gdns. Text 9. Straight ahead. At end of Punderson Gdns turn right. Sharp right onto Hollybush Gdns. Sharp left into Car Park. Proceed under railway arch. This is Poyser St. Cross Cambridge Heath Rd to Bethnal Green Museum of Childhood. Text 10. End.

9 In order to accomplish the division of labour in manufacture more completely, a single branch of production is split up into numerous and to some extent entirely new manufactures, according to the varieties of its raw material or the various forms that the same piece of raw material may assume. Thus in France alone, in the first half of the eighteenth century, over 100 different kinds of silk stuffs were woven, and in Avignon, for instance, it was legally required that 'every apprentice should devote himself to only one sort of fabrication, and should not learn the preparation of several kinds of stuff at once'. The territorial division of labour, which confines special branches of production to special districts of a country, acquires fresh stimulus from the system of manufacture, which exploits all natural peculiarities.

DRESS, 1851
Worn by Queen Victoria. Made of Spitalfields silk, it illustrates the Queen's attempts to encourage the languishing Spitalfields industry.

10 Brides were said to look pretty on their wedding day, as if the magic of the greatest occasion in their lives smoothed away all their faults and gave them beauty. She had looked very nice when she stood in front of the tall looking-glass that morning, nicer than ever before - definitely pretty. And she had been able to believe her mother and her relatives and her bridesmaids when they told her so. Her white satin dress was gathered over half a dozen stiff petticoats which gave her height; the flounce of Honiton lace was as fragile as cobwebs, two white ostrich plumes swept down from the diamond coronet which held her veil, and softened the contour of her face.

9. Karl Marx, op.cit. p.474.
10. Evelyn Anthony, *Victoria*, first published 1959, republished, Sphere Books, 1973, p.92.